Lee Bailey's
Soup Meals

Lee Bailey's
Soup Meals

Main Event Soups in Year-Round Menus

by

Lee Bailey

Photographs by Tom Eckerle
Foreword by Liz Smith

Clarkson N. Potter, Inc./Publishers

This book is lovingly dedicated
to the memory of my good friend
and colleague, Carole Bannett

Design by Rochelle Udell

Assistant, Lauren Libert

Copyright © 1989 by Lee Bailey

Published by Clarkson N. Potter, Inc., 201 East 50th Street,
New York, New York 10022 and distributed by Crown
Publishers, Inc.

CLARKSON N. POTTER, POTTER, and colophon are trademarks
of Clarkson N. Potter, Inc.

Manufactured in Japan

Library of Congress Cataloging-in-Publication Data
Bailey, Lee.
  Lee Bailey's soup meals/by Lee Bailey; photographs by Tom
Eckerle.
  Includes index.
  1. Soups. 2. Menus. I. Eckerle, Tom. II. Title. III. Title:
Soup meals.
TX757.B35 1988
641.8′13—dc19   88-17752
                                                        CIP

ISBN 0-517-56901-9

10 9 8 7 6 5 4 3 2

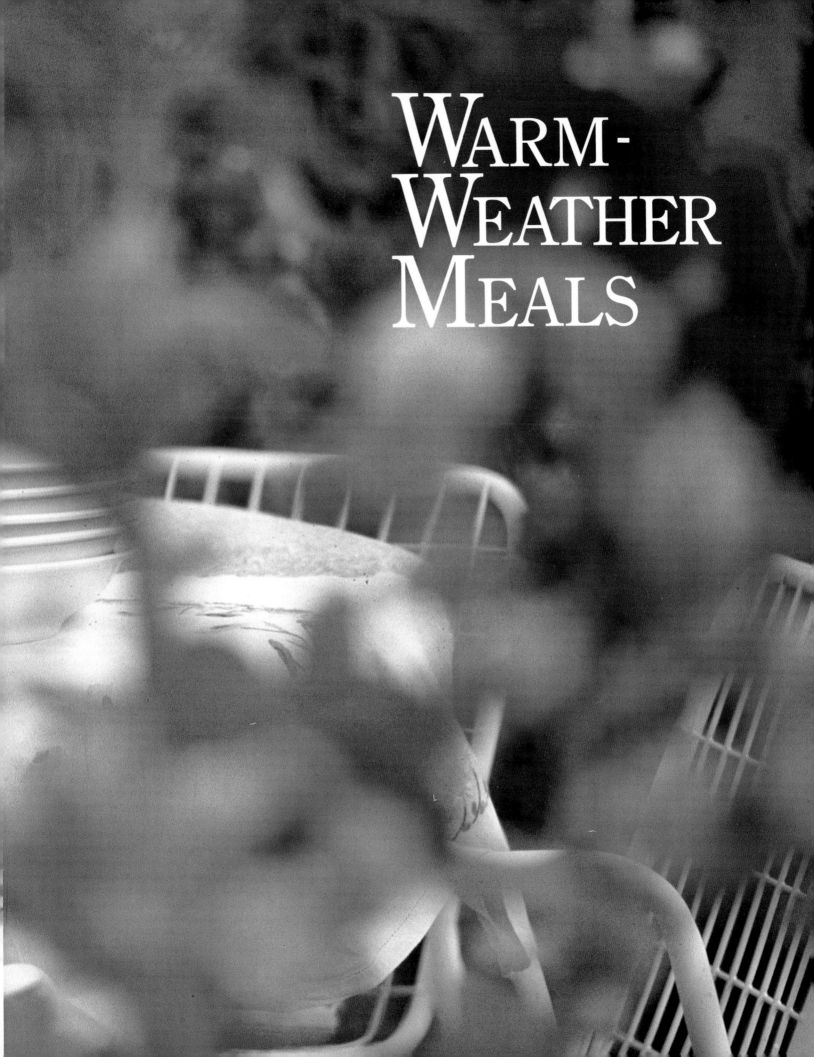

WARM-
WEATHER
MEALS

This book is lovingly dedicated
to the memory of my good friend
and colleague, Carole Bannett

Design by Rochelle Udell
Assistant, Lauren Libert

Copyright © 1989 by Lee Bailey

All rights reserved. No part of this book may be reproduced or
transmitted in any form or by any means, electronic or mechanical,
including photocopying, recording, or by any information storage and
retrieval system, without permission in writing from the publisher.

Published by Clarkson N. Potter, Inc., 201 East 50th Street,
New York, New York 10022 and distributed by Crown
Publishers, Inc.

CLARKSON N. POTTER, POTTER, and colophon are trademarks
of Clarkson N. Potter, Inc.

Manufactured in Japan

Library of Congress Cataloging-in-Publication Data
Bailey, Lee.
  Lee Bailey's soup meals/by Lee Bailey; photographs by Tom
Eckerle.
    Includes index.
    1. Soups. 2. Menus. I. Eckerle, Tom. II. Title. III. Title:
Soup meals.
TX757.B35   1988
641.8′13—dc19   88-17752
                                                          CIP

ISBN 0-517-56901-9

10 9 8 7 6 5 4 3 2

Lee Bailey's
Soup Meals

Main Event Soups in Year-Round Menus

by

Lee Bailey

Photographs by Tom Eckerle
Foreword by Liz Smith

Clarkson N. Potter, Inc./Publishers

Contents

Foreword

The first Mrs. Astor, *the* Mrs. Astor, was a true eccentric. She liked to serve split-second meals at which guests often found the footman clearing their place while they were still lifting fork to lips. Mrs. Astor made herself famous in social circles and infamous in culinary circles by putting down that great masterpiece of the dining art—soup. Mrs. Astor didn't serve soup at her famous dinners, attended by the cream of New York's "400." She even said, "Why would anyone want to put their dinner on top of a lake?!"

Well, all I can say about Mrs. Astor is, what did she know about *love,* having married for money? Soup is a mainstay of civilization. It is a creative synthesis of flavors and textures, served in a comforting, back-to-childhood style; or as a precise and perfectly elegant beginning to the shape of things to come.

It is a thesis of mine that not only do schoolchildren, lumberjacks, deep-sea divers, and opera divas need soup, but freelancers of every stripe cannot live without it. By that I mean writers, artists, inventors, and confined housewives. Lives have often been saved by soup. Just as chicken soup has now been pronounced to indeed be an aid against the common cold, my own happiest memories of being sick as a child center on a vision of my mother approaching the bed with a bowl of steaming tomato soup and some saltines. (I was a true Campbell's kid.) Eventually, of course, I graduated to the tender mercies of the late Henri Soulé and his Le Pavillon, discovering that soup could be more sublime than anything Andy Warhol ever dreamed up.

Now that master of all he touches, Lee Bailey, has decided to tackle another of my favorite subjects. Whatever Lee turns to becomes clearer, better defined, and gains touches of originality and class. Although this is another in his series of better-living-through-the-thrill-of-eating books, I think the most telling story about Lee is of a time when he was retailing his selective styles in trendy Southampton, Long Island. He had a store there that made one's mouth water to buy one of each of the specially chosen or designed Lee Bailey items. One day I went in and discovered a plastic hairbrush which I've been unable to live without ever since.

The brushes lay in heaps of white and heaps of beige. I began to fondle them and asked him, in my garrulous, pointless fashion, "Do these come in other colors?" He looked at me pointedly. Then he said, quietly: "Yes, they come in magenta, forest green, scarlet, mauve, chartreuse, pale pink, baby blue, and sunflower yellow. But," he paused, *"here,* they come only in white and beige!"

That, dear reader, is the essence of my darling, my longtime, my delightful, my practically perfect friend, Lee Bailey. Now he will give us soup—but only in his own selected colors, I'll bet.

LIZ SMITH

Introduction

I've concluded from talking to friends and looking back at my own first years that many of us only come to a true taste and appreciation for soup as adults. For instance, even today, in some remote corner of my mind I still equate cream of tomato soup with feeling feverish and staying home from school, while thoughts of those home-made vegetable soups of my childhood are memorable mostly because of all the corn-bread I consumed with them. And as for gumbo, as much as I genuinely liked its flavor, I always wanted so much rice in mine that the dish became gumbo-flavored rice instead of soup.

And so it went until I was out on my own and rediscovered, first, gumbo, and then vegetable soup (I'm afraid cream of tomato is lost to me forever). Now I've done a complete about-face, counting soup among my favorite foods. And lately as one of my favorite meals. Let me explain.

For a long while, I really thought of soup as something you had as a quick lunch or occasionally for a Sunday supper. I never particularly cared for it one way or another as a first course. However, several years ago I became aware that I was beginning to treat it more as a proper meal and to experiment with various soups that had never interested me before. The upshot is that I began making menus built around soups. These were both for lunches and informal dinners.

There are several advantages here, an obvious one being that soup can be made in advance. When it is the main course, it frees you to indulge in other little flights of culinary fancy which you would perhaps otherwise not bother with—like, for example, a gravlax soufflé as an appetizer. You see what I mean. Or you could whip up a dessert soufflé to finish the meal, since the soufflé is essentially all the *real* cooking you would have to do on the spot.

And, of course, it's a given that soups are nutritious and satisfying. In these days of raised consciousness concerning our health, that's another very real plus.

But thoughts of nutrition aside, many people seem to be rapidly becoming liberated in their eating habits and in what they actually consider a meal to be in the first place. Everyone has read about a growing number of restaurants that specialize in meals composed of many small courses (which the Chinese and Japanese have known about for centuries). Or what of the sudden popularity of tapas—that classic Spanish version of the antipasto approach to dining? No longer, it seems, do people always demand a conventionally structured meal. So probably I was responding to this general mood of liberation myself when I started to alter my concept of how and when soup should be eaten.

Finally, though, who needs reasons? If you like soup, why not make a meal around it instead of just having it as a bridge to the main event or to warm you on a cold winter day? There sure are lots of possibilities here, and once you learn the basics, heaven knows what you might come up with yourself!

A word about how *Soup Meals* is structured. In it you will find warm- and cold-weather menus, for both lunch and dinner,

each built around a particular soup. Many of these are three-course affairs: appetizer, soup, and dessert. And each menu includes a different bread or muffin recipe.

There is also a section called Some Good Salads; these have a bit more personality and in some cases are a bit more complicated than the average little green salad. I envision that you might, on occasion, want to try one of them either after a light soup or instead of the first course.

And since many people think of soup and sandwich as almost one word, I've made a section called Some Good Sandwiches. Obviously these may be used in combination with any of the soups you like.

Finally, although the menus have been put together to be balanced, you shouldn't feel constrained to follow them exactly. So, mix things together that you like the sound of, and in so doing you will greatly multiply the number of menus that may be devised from the recipes here. To illustrate that point you will find chapters entitled Variations on Summer Soup Meals and Variations on Winter Soup Meals. These are structured in such a way as to suggest the many possibilities you may realize from a group of menus. However, all you really need to guide you is your own personal taste.

At the back of the book you will find a few short pages about equipment and sources to round out the whole thing.

As I said at the beginning, get the basics under your belt and you'll be making soup from everything imaginable.

LEE BAILEY
Bridgehampton, Long Island

Asparagus Soup Lunch.

Warm-Weather Meals

As you might imagine, soups that I make in the warm weather are often both lighter in texture and more pronounced in vegetable flavor than the ones I make in cold weather. I leave the dried beans and meat soups to the winter months. Also, proportionately more of my warm-weather soups are served at noon. They can be a marvelous dish to build lunch around, whether the weather is steamy or balmy.

Many of my summer soups contain fresh tomatoes, mainly because I love their flavor so much. But to tell the truth, I've tried to restrain myself on this score because tomatoes can become overpowering and make the soups they are used in taste too much alike. Not a bad thing if you are a tomato lover, but maybe not so good if you are after variety. And as most of us have learned over the years, tomatoes are the one vegetable (fruit, actually) that almost *must* be eaten in season, preferably vine ripened.

Anyway, I am a nut about most other vegetables too, so you can imagine what a field day I have out in the Hamptons when all the produce begins to come in.

As you go through these recipes you will notice that many, especially for soups, list ingredients by weight followed by the number of vegetables required. It was done this way because raw vegetables, particularly in small quantities, are difficult to measure accurately with a conventional measuring cup or spoon.

You will also notice when you make some of the soups in this chapter that they are very thick. This is a personal preference, but if it is one you don't happen to share, by all means thin the soups to the consistency you prefer. In most cases this may be done with anything from chicken stock to skim milk to heavy cream. When doing this, the only thing to remember is to check the seasoning. While it is not likely the soup will require more seasoning when you add chicken stock, the same might not be the case when you substitute milk or cream. And you will notice that if a soup is served very cold, it also will probably require more seasoning. Cold temperatures seem to diminish the potency of most seasonings.

On pages 74–75 in the Cold-Weather section I have given recipes for making Chicken, Beef, and Vegetable Stocks. Following here is a recipe for Fish Stock. While this is not too much trouble to make, especially if you are hanging around the house anyway, I know many people don't want to bother. This resistance is probably truer with fish stock than with other stocks because the average cook doesn't seem to have as many uses for fish stock as for chicken or beef—unless cooks just happen to be particularly partial to fish and seafood.

Luckily, there is a very good fish market near my house where homemade frozen fish stock is sold, so I don't make it often myself. With that in mind, it might be worth the effort to use your Yellow Pages and call local fish markets to see if you can find homemade fish stock ready-made in your locale.

If you do make fish stock, remember that it is an important ingredient of a seafood risotto as well, so you might plan to make a fish soup one week and a seafood risotto the next—since as long as you are going to the trouble to make the stock, you might as well make enough to use for more than one occasion.

The other alternative is to substitute bottled clam juice for fish stock. Frankly, I've never found this too satisfactory in soup. But if you do, be sure to dilute it with water (about half and half) or light chicken stock. As a matter of fact, if I had to choose between clam juice and chicken stock to make a fish soup, I think I'd go for the chicken stock.

Fish Stock

4 pounds fish bones, heads (gills removed), and tails from any nonoily white fish; no bluefish, mackerel, salmon, or the like (see Note)
2 medium onions, coarsely chopped
4 large shallots, coarsely chopped
4 ribs celery with tops, broken into several pieces
3 large carrots, scrubbed but not peeled, broken into several pieces
3 cloves
2 large bay leaves
6 sprigs parsley
1½ teaspoons dried thyme, or a large sprig of fresh
18 peppercorns
2 strips lemon rind
4 cups water
2 cups dry white wine

Wash fish bones, heads, and tails in cold water and place in a large stockpot. Add all other ingredients. Bring quickly to a boil, then reduce heat until liquid is just barely simmering. Cook at this heat level for 20 to 30 minutes, skimming foam as necessary.

Place a double thickness of damp cheesecloth in a colander and pour the stock through it. Allow to drain thoroughly, but do not press down. Discard solids. Allow stock to cool and then refrigerate.

Makes 1½ to 2 quarts

Note: If you have any shrimp, lobster, or crab shells around, these may be added, too.

Asparagus Soup Lunch

When asparagus is in season around here, you seem to have it served steamed and buttered every place you go—which isn't exactly bad—so making soup with it is a nice change. And in the winter, when asparagus appears out of season, soup made from it is just as good as when local asparagus first leaps from the ground.

In this menu, before the soup there is a delicious and very flavorful gravlax mousse with a traditional mustard and dill mayonnaise.

And to munch along with the soup is an assortment of easy-to-prepare breads. Luscious berries and coconut piqued with lemon juice finish it all off.

Menu

Gravlax Mousse with Mustard-Dill Mayonnaise
ASPARAGUS SOUP
Melba Toast, Fried Tortillas, and Toasted Pita Bread Triangles
Strawberries and Lemon Juice with Toasted Coconut
Wine
Iced Tea

Gravlax Mousse with Mustard-Dill Mayonnaise.
Above right: Asparagus Soup. Right: Melba Toast,
Fried Tortillas, and Toasted Pita Bread Triangles.
Far right: Strawberries and Lemon Juice with
Toasted Coconut.

Asparagus Soup Lunch

Gravlax Mousse

You could, of course, make this with smoked salmon or some other oily smoked fish, but I like it best as is. As a change you could flavor the mayonnaise with puréed watercress instead of dill.

- 12 ounces gravlax, cut into ½-inch-wide strips
  Salt to taste
  White pepper to taste
- 1 envelope unflavored gelatin, dissolved in ¼ cup hot water and allowed to cool
- 1½ cups heavy cream

Place gravlax strips in a food processor and purée with the salt and white pepper until smooth, scraping down sides as needed. Add gelatin mixture and process. Pour cream slowly and steadily into the machine while it is running. Stop to scrape down sides if necessary. Spoon mixture into 6 individual small soufflé dishes or ¾-cup molds and refrigerate until set, about 30 to 45 minutes.

To unmold, place cups in a pan of very hot water for a few seconds. Turn onto individual plates. If the mousse is too melted, place in the refrigerator to firm up before serving, about 30 to 45 minutes.

Serve with Mustard-Dill Mayonnaise (recipe follows).

Mustard-Dill Mayonnaise

- ½ cup mayonnaise, preferably homemade (recipe follows)
- ⅓ cup Dijon mustard
- 1 tablespoon tarragon vinegar
- ¼ teaspoon white pepper
- 2 heaping tablespoons chopped fresh dill

Whisk mayonnaise, mustard, vinegar, and white pepper until blended. Fold in dill. Refrigerate until ready to use.

Makes about 1¼ cups

HOMEMADE MAYONNAISE

- 3 tablespoons plus 1 teaspoon fresh lemon juice
- 2 generous teaspoons green peppercorn mustard
- 2 teaspoons salt
- ½ teaspoon white pepper
- 1 egg
- 2 drops Tabasco sauce
- 1½ cups safflower oil
- ½ cup mild olive oil

Put all ingredients except oils into bowl of a food processor fitted with a metal blade. Put top in place and turn on machine. Pour oils into mixture in a steady stream through the feed tube (with the motor still running). Add a few more drops of lemon juice or a bit more salt if necessary. Refrigerate in a covered jar until ready to use. This holds its flavor for 4 or 5 days. It will start to taste a bit metallic after that.

Makes 2½ cups

Asparagus Soup

I think you will find this soup's texture creamy enough with simple chicken stock enhanced by the merest amount of half-and-half, but you certainly could replace part of the stock with skim or regular milk, or light cream. This might cause the finished soup to require a bit more seasoning, so be sure to check it before serving if you decide to do this.

You also could serve this soup at room temperature or only slightly chilled, if you think that would suit you more than the more traditional iced soup. Personally, I eat almost all summer soups that way.

- 1½ pounds fresh asparagus, washed and with tough or dry ends removed
- ¼ cup (½ stick) unsalted butter
- ½ cup chopped onion
- 1 cup carefully washed and chopped leeks (white part only)
- ½ cup chopped celery
- 1 small baking potato (about ½ pound), peeled and cubed

3½ cups chicken stock
1 teaspoon lemon juice
  Salt and white pepper to taste
  Paprika (optional)
½ cup half-and-half

Garnish
  Crème fraîche or whipped cream

Snap off asparagus tips and set the stalks aside. Melt butter in a deep skillet with a cover. Add asparagus tips, onion, leeks, celery, and potato. Cover tightly and cook over the very lowest heat until vegetables are soft, 20 minutes or more.

Meanwhile, place chicken stock in a large saucepan with the reserved asparagus stalks, cut into large pieces. Bring to a boil and simmer, covered tightly, for about 30 minutes. Discard stalks and set stock aside.

In a food processor purée softened vegetables and add to the asparagus stock. Season with lemon juice, salt, white pepper, and paprika, if desired.

Allow to cool and then refrigerate.

Stir in half-and-half and serve garnished with a dollop of crème fraîche or whipped cream and a sprinkling of paprika, if desired.

Serves 6

Melba Toast, Fried Tortillas, and Toasted Pita Bread Triangles

Preheat oven to approximately 250 degrees, or as low as it can be set. Cut slices of very thin white or whole wheat bread in two. Place on cookie sheets and toast until golden. This may take 1 hour or less, depending on how low your oven will go and how dark you like the toast.

Cut corn tortillas into triangles and fry in hot, but not smoking, safflower oil until golden, a minute or so. Drain on paper towels.

Pull pita breads in two and then cut each half into triangles. Place these on a cookie sheet and toast in a 325-degree oven until crisp and golden. Turn once.

Store all of these in an airtight container if you are not planning to use them right away. The melba toast keeps best. Tortillas tend to get a bit tough (but I still like their taste), and the pita gets very hard and dry, which I don't mind but you may.

Strawberries and Lemon Juice with Toasted Coconut

Some people add a dash of framboise to this. Personally, I don't think it is needed, but you could compromise and serve it on the side.

2 pints ripe strawberries, washed, hulled, and cut in half
1 tablespoon lemon juice
1 cup toasted coconut, loosely packed

Toss strawberries with the lemon juice and refrigerate for 30 minutes before serving. Arrange on a platter and sprinkle with the coconut.

Serves 6

Here's How

The first thing you will want to do is make the mousse. You could certainly finish this a day or so in advance. You can also make the basic mayonnaise in advance, but I wouldn't mix the other ingredients into it until just before serving.

If you have time the soup, too, might be made when you prepare the mousse. I'm not exactly sure it makes any difference, but when I do this ahead, I just add about half the liquid (chicken stock or milk) required, saving the balance to stir in when I am ready to serve.

The breads are best toasted (and fried) close to the time they are to be eaten, although they do store well.

And as for the dessert, I'd mix it up just about the time you are ready to sit down to lunch.

As you can see, this gives you plenty of leeway.

Cauliflower and Cress Soup Lunch

Many people think of cauliflower as a fall vegetable—that is certainly when it floods the roadside produce stands in these parts—but luckily, it is available almost year-round. So you can make this soup, which includes cress, anytime you please. It is a real favorite of my friends, so I'm sure you will love it as much as they do.

The meal starts with a fresh-tasting ceviche and ends with a smooth *coeur de crème* and ripe fruit.

Incidentally, the English Muffin Loaf is quite easy to make and is good toasted.

Menu

Red Snapper and Scallop Ceviche
CAULIFLOWER AND CRESS SOUP
English Muffin Loaf
Coeur de Crème with Mixed Fruit
Wine
Iced Tea

Left: Red Snapper and Scallop Ceviche. Above: The complete meal. Right: Cauliflower and Cress Soup. Far right: Coeur de Crème with Mixed Fruit.

Cauliflower and Cress Soup Lunch

Red Snapper and Scallop Ceviche

Almost any mild-flavored fish or seafood may be used for this dish, so if snapper is not available feel free to make a substitute.

    1 pound red snapper fillet, cut into 4 × ½-inch
        (approximate) strips
    1 pound sea scallops, cleaned
    ¾ cup fresh lime juice (about 6 limes)
    1 medium red onion cut into thin rings
    1 medium to large red bell pepper
    2 medium jalapeño peppers (canned), seeded and
        finely diced
    ½ cup finely chopped fresh Italian parsley
    1 cup fresh shredded unsweetened coconut
        (optional)
        Salt and freshly ground black pepper
    ¾ cup good-quality mild olive oil
    2 tablespoons tequila (optional)

Garnish
    1 lime, cut in rings
        Endive leaves

Mix snapper and scallops in a glass container with the lime juice and marinate for at least 4 hours in the refrigerator.

Meanwhile, place red pepper in a pan under the broiler. Turn every so often until the skin completely blackens, then put in a small brown paper bag and close the top. This will trap the moisture as the pepper cools and make it easier to peel. Peel and seed pepper, discarding top. Cut into strips.

Discard fish marinade. In a glass container, layer fish, onions, red pepper strips, jalapeño peppers, parsley, and coconut, if desired. Salt and pepper generously to taste. Mix oil and tequila, and pour over all. Chill. Garnish with fresh lime rings and endive.

Serves 6 to 8

Cauliflower and Cress Soup

There are often a number of different types of peppery cress available in specialty markets in summer. Upland cress, for example, is a kind of cress cultivated in garden soil instead of water, and is a relative of watercress. Some cresses are stronger than others, and almost any one of them will work here. However, I do think the stronger the flavor the better, since cauliflower has a pretty potent taste and the cress should be able to stand up to it.

    1½ generous cups small cauliflower florets
        Low-fat milk
    6 tablespoons (¾ stick) unsalted butter
    ¾ cup finely chopped green onions, including some
        tops
    ¾ teaspoon salt
    1½ generous cups peeled and finely diced potatoes
    2½ cups rich Chicken Stock (page 74)
    8 ounces trimmed cress, heavy stems removed
        Scant ¼ teaspoon white pepper, or to taste

Garnish
    Crème fraîche
    Cress sprigs

In a small saucepan, cover cauliflower with milk and bring to a simmer. Continue to cook until fork-tender, approximately 10 minutes. When done, set aside (in the milk).

Meanwhile, melt butter in a large skillet and add green onions. Sauté over medium-low heat until limp, approximately 5 minutes. Add salt, potatoes, and chicken stock. Bring to a simmer and cover tightly. Cook for 10 minutes.

While stock is cooking, clean and stem the cress. Add to potatoes, cover again, and cook an additional 10 minutes, shaking pan occasionally. Test potatoes for doneness. They should pierce easily with the tines of a fork. Add white pepper. Drain the cauliflower (reserve milk), and add to skillet. Put vegetables in a food processor and purée thoroughly. Return to skillet and add 1 cup of the reserved cauliflower milk. If you do not have enough milk, add plain milk to make up the difference. Heat, and correct seasoning if necessary.

Serve warm but not piping hot. Garnish with crème fraîche and a sprig of cress if you have it handy.

Serves 6

English Muffin Loaf

George Bay of the famous Bay's English Muffins in Chicago had his kitchen create this recipe for me. It is as delicious as their muffins.

- ¼ cup instant mashed potato flakes
- 2 cups milk, scalded
- 2 cakes fresh yeast, or 1 package active dry yeast
- ½ cup warm water (105°–115° F)
  Pinch of sugar
- 6 cups bread flour
- 2 tablespoons sugar
- 1 tablespoon salt
- ¼ cup (½ stick) unsalted butter, melted and cooled
  White cornmeal

Place instant potatoes in a small bowl, add the scalded milk, and stir to dissolve. In another bowl, mash the yeast and add water and sugar. Stir well and set aside.

In a large mixer bowl, combine flour, sugar, and salt. Add the potato mixture, yeast mixture, and butter. Stir with a spatula until flour is moistened. Using a mixer dough hook, knead mixture for 10 minutes. It should form a ball and pull away from the bottom of the container. Place dough in a fresh, buttered bowl. Cover lightly and let rise in a warm place until doubled in volume, about 1 hour.

Thinly butter two 8 × 4-inch loaf pans. Add a small amount of the cornmeal to the pans and rotate to evenly coat the interiors. Knock out any excess. Set aside.

Punch down and divide dough into 2 equal pieces. On a sparingly floured board, roll out one piece of dough into an 8 × 14-inch rectangle. Brush off any excess flour, then roll into a loaf shape, pinching bottom seam to seal. Place dough, seam side down, in prepared pan. Repeat with remaining dough. Cover with plastic wrap and let rise in a warm place until dough extends 2 inches above pan.

Meanwhile, preheat oven to 375 degrees.

Bakes loaves in the oven for 34 to 40 minutes or until golden brown. Loaves should make a hollow sound when tapped. Let cool on a wire rack.

Makes 2 loaves

Coeur de Crème with Mixed Fruit

Mardee Regan, who worked with me on my Country Desserts *book, gave me this recipe, her own variation of classic* coeur de crème. *You'll love it.*

- 8 ounces good-quality cream cheese
- ¾ cup sifted confectioners' sugar
- 1 teaspoon lime juice
- 1 teaspoon grated lemon rind
- 1 teaspoon vanilla extract
- 1 tablespoon framboise *eau-de-vie*
- 1¼ cups heavy cream, whipped

Beat cream cheese with a hand mixer until fluffy, then beat in confectioners' sugar, lime juice, and lemon rind. Mix vanilla and framboise into the whipped cream and then add to cream cheese mixture.

Line a *coeur de crème* mold or a closely woven basket with a double layer of fine cheesecloth. Pour in mixture and smooth top. Cover with a layer of cheesecloth and place the mold or basket on a plate and allow the *coeur de crème* to "weep" in the refrigerator overnight. Discard any liquid, and serve with sweetened fresh fruit.

Serves 6

Here's How

A perfect make-ahead lunch—just the ticket for a busy weekend of entertaining. You could either put it all together a day or so before you want to serve, or you could do it piecemeal whenever you find a spare moment.

When you make the soup, finish it up to the point of adding the reserved milk (but don't add it). Then when you want to serve the soup, heat the milk to almost boiling and stir it into the cauliflower mixture. This should bring the soup to room temperature, which is the way I like this.

Above: Tomato Aspic with Crabmeat Salad. *Below:* Poached Apricots, Pink Peppercorns, and Mint. *Opposite:* Potato and Celery Root Soup with Onion-Parmesan Puffs.

Potato and Celery Root Soup Lunch

Potato and Celery Root Soup Lunch

Celery root usually begins showing up in our local markets at the end of the summer, so I guess technically this could be called an Indian summer lunch, for one of those last clear and warm days before we head into the cold wind.

It begins with an old Southern favorite, tomato aspic, and ends with a simple dessert of poached fruit. All in all, pretty satisfying.

Menu

> *Tomato Aspic with Crabmeat Salad*
> *POTATO AND CELERY ROOT SOUP*
> *Onion-Parmesan Puffs*
> *Poached Apricots, Pink Peppercorns, and*
> *Mint with Crème Fraîche*
> *Wine*
> *Iced Tea*

Tomato Aspic with Crabmeat Salad

I've often wondered why tomato aspic never became a traditional dish in any part of the United States except the South. I have probably eaten half my weight in it over the years and still love it—even though lots of people seem to think of it as being rather "tea-roomy."

I serve it with crabmeat, but any mayonnaise-dressed concoction (tuna, chicken) could be substituted.

1½ envelopes unflavored gelatin
½ cup cold water
3½ cups crushed canned tomatoes or canned tomato pulp, coarsely chopped
3 tablespoons grated onion
3 tablespoons grated green bell pepper
1 teaspoon Worcestershire sauce
2 dashes Tabasco
2 tablespoons red wine vinegar or fresh lemon juice
¼ teaspoon black pepper
1½ teaspoons salt, or to taste
3 cups picked-over fresh crabmeat, chilled
Homemade Mayonnaise (page 6)
Lemon juice

Sprinkle gelatin over water in a saucer. Meanwhile, heat crushed tomatoes in a saucepan. Stir softened gelatin into the tomatoes off the heat. Add onion, green pepper, Worcestershire sauce, Tabasco, vinegar or lemon juice, pepper, and salt. Mix thoroughly and pour into a 6-cup ring mold. Refrigerate for several hours, or until thoroughly set.

To serve, loosen the aspic by placing the mold briefly in a pan of hot water. Then turn it onto a serving plate, making sure it is centered. Re-refrigerate until it has set again.

Toss the crabmeat with the mayonnaise and a bit of lemon juice, and heap into the middle of the aspic ring. The crabmeat salad should not be too seasoned because the aspic is very spicy.

Serves 6 to 8

Potato and Celery Root Soup

You might want to try experimenting with this basic potato soup recipe. I think you will find that potatoes combine wonderfully with almost any kind of flavor, from watercress to sweet squash. You can hardly go wrong, so use your imagination.

2 tablespoons (¼ stick) unsalted butter
1 medium onion, coarsely chopped
1 large shallot, coarsely chopped
2 very large leeks, carefully washed and cut into 1-inch rings (with some green)
1 rib celery, coarsely chopped
2 medium baking potatoes, peeled and cut into medium cubes (about 3 cups)
1 small celery root, peeled and cut into medium to small cubes (about 1½ cups)
1 teaspoon salt
½ teaspoon white pepper
4 cups rich Chicken Stock (page 74), heated

Melt butter in a deep saucepan and sauté onion and shallot over medium heat until onions begin to turn brown, about 5 minutes. Add leeks and celery. Cover tightly and sweat for 15 minutes over very low heat.

Add potatoes, celery root, salt, pepper, and 1½ cups of the stock to the saucepan. Bring to a boil and simmer, uncovered, for 10 minutes or more, until potatoes and celery root are fork-tender.

Transfer soup mixture to a food processor and purée until smooth. Return to the saucepan and add the balance of the stock. Simmer for a few minutes, then correct seasoning if necessary. Serve medium hot.

Serves 6

Onion-Parmesan Puffs

Considering how impressive these little puffs look, they are remarkably easy to prepare. It just takes a few minutes of elbow grease to mix the ingredients.

> 1½ cups water
> ¾ cup (1½ sticks) unsalted butter
> 2 cups coarsely chopped onions
> 2 teaspoons salt
> 1½ cups all-purpose flour
> 6 eggs
> 1 cup freshly grated Parmesan cheese
> Milk
> Additional grated Parmesan for topping

Preheat oven to 400 degrees and grease 2 cookie sheets.

Bring water to a boil in a medium saucepan and add ½ cup (1 stick) of the butter. Meanwhile, sauté the onions in the remaining butter until wilted, about 5 minutes. Set aside.

When butter has melted in the water and mixture has come to a boil again, add salt and flour, all at once. Turn the heat down to low and stir for a few minutes until the mixture makes a ball and pulls away from the sides of the pan. Off the heat, beat in the eggs one at the time, mixing well after each addition. Combine the Parmesan cheese with the dough and then the sautéed onions, mixing thoroughly.

Drop heaping tablespoons of dough onto the greased cookie sheets. Brush tops with milk and then sprinkle with additional Parmesan cheese. Bake until golden and puffy, about 35 to 40 minutes.

Makes about 2 dozen puffs

Poached Apricots, Pink Peppercorns, and Mint with Crème Fraîche

I never serve fresh apricots unless it is at the very height of their season for, like peaches, they are often mealy when they have not been allowed to ripen naturally—and I think there is nothing worse.

> 2 cups water
> 2 tablespoons pink peppercorns
> 1½ cups sugar
> 18 to 24 ripe apricots, depending on size
> 4 sprigs mint, tied (optional)
> Crème fraîche or Devonshire cream

Bring water to a boil and add peppercorns. Simmer for a few minutes, then add sugar. When sugar is well dissolved, add apricots. Cook until just tender; the time will vary according to the size and age of the fruit, but use the point of a sharp knife to test for doneness.

Remove the apricots with a slotted spoon, place in a bowl, and bury the mint in the fruit. Pour the syrup and peppercorns over, then allow to cool. Discard mint and refrigerate fruit.

Serve the apricots with crème fraîche or Devonshire (clotted) cream.

Serves 6

Here's How

Make the soup and the aspic (along with the mayonnaise to combine with the crabmeat) a day or so in advance. The apricots can be poached ahead of time as well. This only leaves the puffs to cook at the last minute, since they are really best served hot.

If you are pressed for time, serve Parmesan Toast (page 39) and save the puffs for when you are more relaxed.

Sorrel Soup Lunch

Left: The table setting. Top: Sorrel Soup.
Above: Corn and Ham Fritters with Tomato Coulis.
Right: Puffy Peach Cake with Bourbon Cream.

Sorrel Soup Lunch

Some versions of sorrel soup are made simply from the vegetable, an onion or two, and stock or cream. While I like it that way, it can be a little biting for my taste, so I use this version, which includes a few potatoes.

The first course is corn and ham fritters with a tomato coulis. This tomato sauce is good on many things, from pasta to a cheese soufflé.

Finally, the peach dessert is a fast, simple little tart-like sweet to finish a meal.

Menu

Corn and Ham Fritters with Tomato Coulis
SORREL SOUP
Cheese Wafers
Puffy Peach Cake with Bourbon Cream
Wine
Iced Tea

Corn and Ham Fritters with Tomato Coulis

I grew up on fritters, but for some reason (maybe it's the oil that has to be dealt with after you are finished) they don't seem to be served much these days. Whatever, I think they are worth the trouble.

1½ cups all-purpose flour
2 teaspoons baking powder
1 teaspoon salt
2 tablespoons (¼ stick) unsalted butter, melted
2 eggs, lightly beaten
   Milk
⅓ cup sliced and shredded prosciutto
1 cup fresh corn kernels, cut from the cob
   Safflower oil for frying

Mix dry ingredients in a bowl. Make a well in the center and pour in butter and eggs. Blend well, then add a few tablespoons of milk. Mix well; the dough should be smooth but not runny, and you should only just be able to shake the batter from the spoon. Keep adding milk and mixing until you reach this consistency. Stir in prosciutto and corn.

Drop the batter by generous tablespoonsful into hot, but not smoking, oil and cook, turning gently until dark

golden; do not let burn. Test one fritter first before going on with the others to make sure you are cooking it the right length of time. You don't want them to be cooked on the outside and underdone in the middle.

Drain fritters on paper towels, then place in a warm oven until you have finished the lot. Serve with Tomato Coulis (recipe follows).

Makes 12 or more fritters

TOMATO COULIS

2 large ripe tomatoes, peeled, seeded, and finely chopped
2 tablespoons balsamic vinegar
1 teaspoon salt
½ teaspoon white pepper
1 tablespoon chopped fresh basil

Toss ingredients together in a bowl and allow to marinate for about 1 hour before serving.

Makes about 1½ cups

Sorrel Soup

Here it is—sorrel soup my way.

3 tablespoons unsalted butter
1 pound onions, coarsely chopped
1 small garlic clove, minced
6 cups Chicken Stock (page 74)
½ pound red potatoes, peeled and coarsely diced
12 ounces trimmed sorrel leaves, torn into large pieces
   Salt and pepper to taste
   Sour cream

Heat butter in a deep pot and sauté onions until wilted and turning golden, about 5 minutes. Add garlic and cook for another minute. Add chicken stock and heat, then add potatoes. Simmer until potatoes are done, about 10 minutes. Stir in sorrel and heat thoroughly.

Transfer mixture to a food processor and purée. Return to the heat and cook for another few minutes, correcting seasoning with salt and pepper if necessary.

Serve with a dollop of sour cream on top of each serving.

Serves 6

Cheese Wafers

I like the flavor of cheese with sorrel soup. Maybe this is only because cheese is strong enough to hold its own with the sorrel.

1 cup grated Swiss cheese
¼ cup grated Parmesan cheese
½ cup (1 stick) unsalted butter, softened
1 teaspoon salt
½ teaspoon freshly ground white pepper
1 cup all-purpose flour

Preheat oven to 350 degrees.

In a large bowl, cream the cheeses and butter. Stir in salt and white pepper. Mix flour in thoroughly until you can make a ball. Divide dough in half, then keep dividing in half until you have 32 small balls, rolling them with your hands. Place the balls about 2 inches apart on an ungreased cookie sheet and flatten slightly.

Bake for 15 minutes, or until golden. Remove with a spatula to a cooling rack.

Makes 32 wafers

Puffy Peach Cake with Bourbon Cream

You can also make this with apples or pears, or a combination of fruit. Vanilla ice cream could be substituted for the bourbon cream.

1 cup sugar, plus additional for topping
½ cup (1 stick) unsalted butter, softened
2 large eggs
1 cup all-purpose flour
1 teaspoon baking powder
  Pinch of salt
4 or more large peaches, peeled, pitted, and quartered lengthwise
1½ tablespoons fresh lemon juice
1 teaspoon ground cinnamon
1 cup heavy cream, whipped and flavored with several tablespoons bourbon

Preheat oven to 350 degrees. Butter an 8-inch square baking dish or an 8- or 9-inch round springform pan. Set aside.

Cream the sugar and the butter until fluffy, about 5 minutes. Beat in eggs thoroughly, one at a time. Set aside.

Sift flour, baking powder, and salt together. Add to the creamed mixture ¼ cup at a time, mixing well after each addition. Pour into prepared pan. Arrange peaches in a regular pattern over all, so the slices are just touching. Sprinkle with the lemon juice. Mix cinnamon with several tablespoons of sugar and sprinkle this on top.

Bake until cake is golden and fluffy, about 1 hour. The fruit will sink into the batter, so don't be alarmed.

Serve warm if you can, although this is not really a necessity. Top with bourbon-flavored whipped cream.

Serves 6

Here's How

Make the soup and the coulis the day before if you like. When I do this, I usually don't add all the stock or cream until it is almost time for the soup to be served.

If the dessert is not going to be served warm, make it any time on the day it is to be served. (You could always warm it a little in a microwave oven.)

As for the wafers, I like them made just before serving—and of course the fritters are best right out of the pot.

Above: Shrimp, White Beans, and Roasted Red Peppers. *Below:* Champagne Grapes with Cheeses. *Opposite:* Zucchini and Butternut Squash Soup.

Zucchini and Butternut Squash Soup Lunch

Zucchini and Butternut Squash Soup Lunch

This lunch is typical of the kind I often serve when the weather is hot and I know I'm going to have a number of meals to prepare. Most of it can be made ahead of time and be put out whenever you are ready. I have used weight measurements here because the proportions are very important, and the flavor will be better. However, if you don't have a home scale, I have given equivalents, but keep in mind they are less accurate.

Muffins are best eaten right out of the oven, but they are so easy to stir up they don't really seem much like cooking. If even this is more than you want to do, substitute something like the Cayenne Wafers (page 26), which can also be made in advance.

Obviously, you could substitute any sort of fruit for the Champagne grapes.

Menu

Shrimp, White Beans, and Roasted Red Peppers
ZUCCHINI AND BUTTERNUT
SQUASH SOUP
Fresh Corn Muffins
Champagne Grapes with Cheeses
Wine
Iced Tea

Shrimp, White Beans, and Roasted Red Peppers

I don't know why these flavors seem to complement one another so well, but they do. I am very fond of this combination and use it often. Try it.

    2 cups dried white (navy) beans
    1 medium onion, coarsely chopped
    1 large garlic clove, minced
    1 large bay leaf
    ¼ teaspoon dried leaf thyme
      Salt and black pepper to taste
    2 tablespoons olive oil
2 or 3 large red bell peppers (or a combination of red
      and yellow), roasted, peeled, and cut into strips
   30 cooked medium shrimp, peeled but with the tails
      left on

Garnish
    Lemon wedges

Soak the beans in water overnight or use the Quick-Soak Method (see Note).

Cover beans with several inches of fresh water. Bring to a simmer and add onion, garlic, bay leaf, and thyme. Simmer, skimming off foam, until water is reduced and beans begin to get tender, about 1 hour. Add more hot water in small amounts if necessary, to keep beans covered. When beans are done, season with salt and pepper, remove bay leaf, and stir in the olive oil.

To serve, place warm beans in a bowl on a large platter. Surround beans with strips of roasted pepper. Sprinkle these with additional olive oil and grind black pepper over all. Arrange cooked shrimp on the side of the platter or around the bowl.

Each serving should have a bit of all the ingredients.

Serves 6

Note: Use the Quick-Soak Method as follows: Place beans in a large pot. Add enough water to cover by 1 inch. Bring to a boil over high heat; turn back to a simmer and cook for 2 minutes. Remove from heat and allow to soak for 1 hour. Drain and return to the pot.

Zucchini and Butternut Squash Soup

Many combinations of summer vegetables work well when puréed together. For my money, one of the best flavor combinations is the slight sweetness of butternut squash when added to zucchini.

    ¼ cup (½ stick) unsalted butter, or half butter and
      half margarine
    8 ounces coarsely chopped, well-washed leeks
      (white part only) (about 2 cups)
    4 ounces coarsely chopped onions
    3 ounces grated carrots (about 1 cup)
    1 small garlic clove, cut into several pieces
    1 teaspoon sugar
    1 ½-pound butternut squash, split and seeded, the
      cut surface rubbed with a little butter
    1 pound trimmed zucchini, cut into large rings
    5 cups rich Chicken Stock (page 74)
      Generous ¼ teaspoon white pepper
    1 teaspoon salt
      Scant ¼ teaspoon ground coriander
      Yogurt (optional)

Preheat oven to 375 degrees.

Melt butter in a large, deep pot with a lid and add leeks, onions, carrots, and garlic. Toss well, then sprinkle sugar over all and cover tightly. Sweat over the lowest possible heat for 20 minutes. Do not allow to burn.

Place butternut squash in a foil-lined pie pan and bake until fork-tender, about 30 to 40 minutes.

When the vegetables in the pot are cooked, add zucchini and 2 cups of the stock plus the white pepper, salt, and coriander. Cook, uncovered, over medium heat until zucchini is very soft, about 10 minutes. Transfer vegetables and liquid to a food processor. Scoop out the pulp of the squash, making sure you get it all, and add to processor mixture. Purée everything together and return to pot. Stir in the balance of the stock and heat. Correct seasoning if necessary. Serve with a dollop of yogurt on top of each serving, if desired.

Serves 6 to 8

Fresh Corn Muffins

Try adding caraway seeds to this for a change. You'll like the result.

>   2 cups white cornmeal
> ½ cup all-purpose flour
> 3½ teaspoons baking powder
> ½ teaspoon baking soda
> 1½ teaspoons salt
> 1½ cups buttermilk
>   2 eggs, lightly beaten
>   2 tablespoons (¼ stick) unsalted butter, melted
>   3 cups fresh corn kernels, cut from the cob

Preheat oven to 450 degrees. Grease two 12-cup muffin tins. Set aside.

Sift together the cornmeal, flour, baking powder, baking soda, and salt. Stir in the buttermilk and then the eggs. Do not overmix. Add butter and corn, then stir just enough to blend. Fill prepared cups and bake for 25 minutes.

Makes approximately 18 to 24 muffins, depending on the size of cups

Champagne Grapes with Cheeses

Champagne grapes are a particular favorite of mine, and I look forward to their brief season at the end of the summer. They are very small, sweet, and seedless— and worth the wait.

A very simple and quick dessert is to put out a bowl of these little beauties atop a bed of cracked ice and serve along with several good cheeses. Try a chèvre and maybe something soft with a bloomy white rind. Camembert, the old standby, is one such.

Incidentally, one of the best investments I ever made was a pair of grape scissors. For the longest time I considered them just one more essentially unnecessary thing to deal with, but they really do their work—grape stems being too difficult to break comfortably without a little help.

Here's How

As I've said, this is really one of those make-ahead meals. All the courses, except for the muffins, can be prepared the day before they are to be served. So the timing is up to you.

The one thing to remember, since everything will most likely be refrigerated, is to take the food out of the refrigerator in plenty of time for it to come to the right temperature. In the case of the beans, this could be several hours. Better too warm than too cold is my motto.

Spinach Soup Lunch

I have put this soup in the Warm-Weather section because the spring and early fall is when I usually make it; however, in truth it could be made year-round, spinach being one of the few leafy green vegetables that never seems to go out with the changing seasons.

To begin the lunch is a fine combination of corn and prosciutto—it's easy, and a pleasant variation to serve in the early fall when the corn is plentiful but you have had your fill of it on the cob.

As for the dessert—just look at the picture.

Menu

Fresh Corn and Prosciutto
SPINACH SOUP
Cayenne Wafers
Raspberry Pie
Wine
Iced Tea

<u>Left</u>: Spinach Soup with Cayenne Wafers.
<u>Top</u>: Fresh Corn and Prosciutto.
<u>Below</u>: Raspberry Pie.

Spinach Soup Lunch

Fresh Corn and Prosciutto

Usually fresh corn has enough milk in it when you scrape the cob that you don't need to add more than butter, salt, and pepper. But if that is not the case, milk or cream may be needed.

>   2 tablespoons (¼ stick) unsalted butter
>   8 to 10 ears fresh corn, kernels cut from the cobs
>   and the cobs scraped with back of a knife
>   1 tablespoon milk or cream (optional)
>   Salt to taste
>   1 teaspoon sugar (optional)
>   3 ounces thin-sliced prosciutto, cut into thin strips

Melt butter in a large skillet, and when bubbling, toss in the corn kernels and corn milk. Stir in milk or cream, if using, and cook over very low heat for several minutes. The corn should be just barely done; this timing will vary with the age and variety of corn used. Sprinkle mixture with salt and sugar, if desired, and mix. Toss in the strips of ham and cook just a few seconds to warm them.

Serves 6

Spinach Soup

The recipe for this marvelously strong-flavored soup came to me from Mary Allen of Roxbury, Connecticut. The only time-consuming thing about it is stemming the spinach; the rest is a breeze. Just make sure the spinach is well washed, as it tends to be sandy and the merest hint of sand ruins it for me.

>   3 pounds fresh spinach, large stems removed and
>   leaves carefully washed
>   ¼ cup (½ stick) unsalted butter
>   1½ cups finely chopped onions
>   2 cups rich Chicken Stock (page 74)
>   2 cups low-fat milk
>   Salt and pepper to taste
>   Dash of grated nutmeg (optional)

Garnish
>   6 thin lemon slices
>   Chopped fresh chives

Place spinach in a large pot with just the water clinging to the leaves. Cover and cook over high heat until wilted and tender.

Meanwhile, melt butter in a large skillet and sauté the onions until golden.

Drain the spinach, reserving the liquid, and place spinach in a food processor along with the onions. Purée until smooth. Combine the puréed spinach-onion mixture with the stock, spinach pan juice, and milk. Slowly bring to a simmer. Add salt and pepper to taste, and a dash of nutmeg, if desired.

Float a thin round of lemon on top of each serving and sprinkle with chopped chives.

Serves 6

Cayenne Wafers

Different versions of these little biscuits are served all over the South, using different kinds of cheese—with and without pepper.

>   1 cup grated sharp cheddar cheese
>   ¼ cup (½ stick) margarine, softened
>   ¼ cup (½ stick) unsalted butter, softened
>   1 teaspoon salt
>   Scant ¼ teaspoon cayenne (ground red) pepper
>   1 cup all-purpose flour

Preheat oven to 350 degrees.

Cream the cheese, margarine, butter, salt, and cayenne in a large bowl. Add the flour and mix thoroughly. Roll into a ball and wrap tightly in plastic wrap. Refrigerate for 30 minutes.

Divide dough in half, then keep dividing the dough in half until you have 32 small balls. Place them on an ungreased cookie sheet and flatten with the heel of the hand. These do not spread out or rise much during baking, so they can be placed fairly close together.

Bake until just golden, about 15 minutes. Allow to cool for just a minute before removing with a spatula to a cooling rack.

These wafers can be kept for several weeks in a tightly closed tin.

Makes 32 biscuits

Raspberry Pie

I'm very fond of this pie because it uses cooked and un-cooked berries together (also an inspiration of Mary Allen). Incidentally, the crust is made from Mrs. Cash-dollar's famous recipe in Country Desserts.

Hot-water Crust
1½ cups solid vegetable shortening
½ cup boiling water
2 tablespoons milk
2 teaspoons salt
4 cups sifted all-purpose flour

Filling
3 pints fresh raspberries, approximately
1 cup sugar
3 tablespoons cornstarch
½ cup water
1 tablespoon unsalted butter

Garnish
1 cup heavy cream, whipped and flavored with 1
teaspoon vanilla extract

To make the crust, place the shortening in a bowl and pour the boiling water over it. Stir until smooth, then add the milk and salt. Place flour in the bowl of a food processor fitted with the plastic blade, and pour the shortening mixture over it. Process until the dough forms a mass. Form into a ball, flatten slightly between 2 sheets of wax paper, and refrigerate for at least 1 hour. This will make enough dough for two 2-crust pies. Divide the dough into 4 equal portions. Use one portion for this pie and freeze the others to use later. This dough keeps very well.

When you are ready to assemble the pie, preheat the oven to 425 degrees. Roll out the dough on a floured surface and line a 9-inch pie pan with it, crimping the edges. Pierce crust with the tines of a fork and then line with foil. Cover bottom of the pan with dried beans or pie weights and bake crust until set, about 5 to 7 minutes. Remove foil and beans. Bake until golden, another 10 minutes. Carefully loosen edges of crust. When almost cool, slide out of pan onto a serving plate if you like, or serve the pie from the pan. Set aside.

Mash enough berries to fill 1 cup. Combine with the sugar, cornstarch, and water in a small saucepan and cook over medium heat, stirring constantly, until the mixture comes to a boil. Continue cooking for about 2 minutes over low heat until the mixture is thickened and clear. Stir in the butter and cook until melted, then allow to cool slightly.

Place the remaining uncooked berries in the baked crust, saving a few perfect ones for a garnish. Pour the cooked berry mixture over the uncooked berries in the crust. Shake gently so glaze seeps down around the raw berries.

Chill pie for a few hours, then top with the flavored whipped cream and garnish with the reserved whole berries.

Serves 6

Here's How

Make the soup a day or so before you will serve it. It will probably separate a bit, but a quick stir will take care of that. Also make, but do not bake, the pie crust the day before.

You could do the wafers as well as finish the pie a few hours before serving.

Cut the corn off the cob about the time the guests are due to arrive, and have it ready for its brief cooking.

Above: Corn Cob Soup and Hot-Water Soda Wafers with Chives. *Below:* Blueberry Shortcake.
Opposite: Gorgonzola Soufflé.

Corn Cob Soup Dinner

Here is a good, old down-home soup dinner that begins with a glamorous soufflé—a nice contrast.

Using corn cobs to make the stock for this soup is a traditional method and is supposed to give the soup a stronger corn flavor. Whatever their effect on the final dish, this is a mighty pleasing soup, although it is not strictly traditional.

The Gorgonzola soufflé is a delightful way to begin the meal and the blueberry shortcake a delicious way to finish it.

Menu

Gorgonzola Soufflé with Cucumber Sauce
CORN COB SOUP
Hot-Water Soda Wafers with Chives
Blueberry Shortcake
Wine
Coffee

Corn Cob Soup Dinner

Gorgonzola Soufflé with Cucumber Sauce

Gorgonzola cheese has a pleasingly tangy flavor and is perfect topped with cucumber sauce.

A light tarragon sauce would make a fine substitute for the cucumber.

    ¼ cup (½ stick) unsalted butter
    3 tablespoons all-purpose flour
    1 cup milk
    1 teaspoon green peppercorn mustard
    1 teaspoon salt
    ¼ teaspoon cayenne (ground red) pepper
    2 cups mild Gorgonzola cheese, cubed
    6 egg yolks
    8 egg whites
    ¼ teaspoon cream of tartar
      Grated Parmesan cheese for dusting soufflé dish

Put a kettle of water on to heat over low heat.

Melt the butter in a medium saucepan over medium heat. Add the flour and mix well. Slowly whisk in the milk and cook until thickened, whisking constantly. Stir in mustard, salt, cayenne, and cheese. Blend well. Beat egg yolks in a small bowl and warm them with a little of the cheese mixture before whisking them in, in a slow steady stream. Cook just a few minutes before allowing to cool.

Beat egg whites until foamy, sprinkle cream of tartar over all, and beat until stiff but not dry. Butter generously a 6-cup or a 2-quart soufflé dish and dust with grated Parmesan cheese, or use 6 similarly prepared individual soufflé dishes.

In a large bowl, fold beaten egg whites into the cheese mixture with an over-and-under motion. Mix just until all white streaks disappear. Pour into prepared soufflé dish. Sprinkle the top with grated Parmesan cheese if you like.

Put soufflé dish in a larger pan and surround with boiling water. Place in a cold oven and turn on to 325 degrees. Bake until puffy and brown, about 50 minutes.

Serve immediately with a little Cucumber Sauce (recipe follows).

Serves 6 generously

CUCUMBER SAUCE

    1 large English cucumber (about 1 pound), peeled,
      seeded, and coarsely chopped
    2 tablespoons tarragon vinegar
    1 tablespoon safflower oil
    ½ cup Chicken Stock (page 74)
    2 tablespoons very finely chopped red onion
    1 tablespoon chopped fresh lemon thyme or parsley
    1 teaspoon salt
    ¼ teaspoon white pepper

Purée the cucumber, vinegar, oil, and stock. Whisk in the other ingredients. Do not refrigerate.

Makes approximately 1½ cups

Corn Cob Soup

    2 pounds smoked pork neck, cut into several large
      pieces (see Note)
    3 quarts water (see Note)
    4 large ribs celery, broken into pieces
    1 large bay leaf
    2 large carrots, broken into several pieces
    6 large sprigs parsley
   12 ears corn, kernels cut off and milk scraped from
      cobs; 6 scraped cobs reserved
    2 tablespoons safflower oil
    2 tablespoons all-purpose flour
    1 cup coarsely chopped green onions, with some
      tops
    ½ cup coarsely chopped shallots
    1 large red bell pepper, coarsely chopped
    1 large garlic clove, minced
    2 pounds ripe tomatoes, peeled, seeded, and cut
      into large chunks
 1½ teaspoons salt, or to taste
    ½ teaspoon white pepper, or to taste
    1 teaspoon paprika

In a large pot, cover neck pieces with water and add celery, bay leaf, carrots, and parsley. Break the reserved scraped corn cobs in half and add to pot. Bring to a simmer and continue to cook very slowly for 2 hours, skimming foam when necessary.

Pour mixture through a strainer, discarding the neck meat and bones as well as the vegetables (or make a sandwich spread of the meat—it will need a bit of seasoning). Carefully remove all fat. Set aside.

Heat safflower oil in a deep pot and add flour. Make a roux by cooking until mixture is golden. Scrape from the bottom of pan with spatula to keep from getting too brown. Add green onions, shallots, and red pepper. Mix and then sauté until vegetables are wilted, about 5 minutes. Do not burn.

Measure out 8 cups of the degreased stock (this should be about what you have) and pour into pot. If you don't have quite enough, add chicken stock to make up the difference. Mix thoroughly. Add garlic and tomatoes, and simmer for 30 minutes. Skim foam if necessary.

Pour mixture through a strainer and catch the solids. Put them into a food processor and purée. Return the strained liquid and purée to the pot; stir in corn kernels with their milk. Add salt, white pepper, and paprika. Simmer for 5 minutes, just long enough to cook corn.

Serve slightly warmed or at room temperature.

Serves 8

Note: You can also make the stock essence by using chicken stock instead of water and 1½ pounds of smoked pork shin or smoked ham hocks instead of smoked neck.

Hot-Water Soda Wafers with Chives

These tend to toughen up if allowed to sit around too long, so they are best eaten shortly after baking.

1½ cups water
1 teaspoon salt
¼ cup (½ stick) unsalted butter
½ teaspoon baking soda
2 cups all-purpose flour
3 or more tablespoons chopped fresh chives

Preheat oven to 425 degrees.

Place water, salt, and butter in a medium saucepan and bring to a boil. Meanwhile, toss baking soda and flour together. When water is boiling, add flour all at once, stirring constantly with a wooden spoon. Continue to stir over low heat for another minute, until the mixture is well combined and has formed a ball.

Pull off walnut-size pieces of dough and quickly roll each into a ball. Flatten slightly and sprinkle with chives. Place on an ungreased cookie sheet and press with heel of the hand until very thin. Prick with a fork in several places. Continue until all dough is used.

Bake for 15 minutes or until browned and crisp. Allow to cool slightly on a rack.

Makes approximately 48 wafers

Blueberry Shortcake

I love the old-fashioned shortcake biscuits called for here —so will you.

2 cups sifted all-purpose flour
2½ teaspoons baking powder
¼ teaspoon salt
1 tablespoon sugar
½ cup (1 stick) cold butter, cut into bits
½ cup light cream or half-and-half
1½ pints fresh blueberries
Sugar to taste
Vanilla-flavored whipped cream

Preheat oven to 450 degrees.

Sift the flour, baking powder, salt, and sugar into a large bowl. Cut the butter in with a pastry blender or 2 knives. Pour cream in all at once, and stir quickly until dough leaves sides of bowl.

Turn out onto a floured surface and dust top lightly with additional flour. Roll out the dough with a floured pin to a 1-inch thickness. Cut into 8 large biscuits and bake on an ungreased cookie sheet until golden, about 8 to 10 minutes.

While the biscuits are baking, mash a few berries in a bowl and add sugar to your taste. Toss with other whole berries.

When biscuits are done, split and butter each half. Arrange biscuit bottoms on individual plates. Pile berries on each and place a dab of whipped cream on the berries. Add the biscuit tops and more berries and cream if you like.

Serves 8

Here's How

Make the soup completely the day before, or prepare the stock for the soup several days in advance if you have the fresh corn cobs, and then finish it later. You can also make the cucumber sauce the day before.

Bake the biscuits in the afternoon of the day they will be eaten and get the berries and cream ready about the time guests are due to arrive.

Organize the ingredients for the soufflé and wafers so they can be done quickly; as a matter of fact, you might make the soufflé base so it will be finished and cooling when the guests arrive.

If you think making these wafers is too much trouble, substitute Melba Toast (page 7).

Curried Shrimp and Potato Soup Dinner

The inspiration for this curried shrimp soup is a shrimp dish my maternal grandmother used to make. Her family came to Louisiana from South Carolina in the early eighteenth century, and family lore has it that the shrimp dish was a favorite from the Carolina days—without the curry. I don't know when the curry got in there. This soup also could be made with crab or lobster, or even a combination of seafood.

A dish of fresh asparagus is a fine way to begin a meal, and this time they are topped with a warm vinaigrette. If that seems too tedious to bother with, use any vinaigrette you like, but try the warm vinaigrette some other time. It's good.

The skillet pepper bread was inspired by an East Indian method of preparing bread, and it seemed fitting to serve it with the curried shrimp.

The peppermint pears were inspired by the fact that I love the taste of peppermint.

So this probably tells you more than you care to know about my inspirations.

Opposite, top: Asparagus with Warm Tomato Vinaigrette. Opposite, bottom: Curried Shrimp and Potato Soup. Above: The entire soup meal, including Skillet Pepper Bread. Below: Peppermint Pear.

Menu

Asparagus with Warm Tomato Vinaigrette
CURRIED SHRIMP AND POTATO SOUP
Skillet Pepper Bread
Peppermint Pears with
Pecan–Brown Sugar Shortbread
Wine
Coffee

Curried Shrimp and Potato Soup Dinner

Asparagus with Warm Tomato Vinaigrette

This warm vinaigrette is very good on fresh little boiled (unpeeled) new red potatoes as well as steamed fresh cauliflower—or what about a combination of the two tossed with a little crumbled crisp bacon?

¼ cup finely chopped shallots
¼ cup olive oil
1 cup peeled, seeded, and chopped vine-ripened
  tomatoes
¼ cup red wine vinegar
1 large garlic clove, finely minced
⅔ cup dry white wine
¼ teaspoon salt
  Freshly ground black pepper to taste
18 to 24 medium to large asparagus, steamed until
  crisp-tender

Sauté the shallots in the oil over medium heat until wilted but not browned, about 5 minutes. Add the tomatoes and bring to a simmer. Cook for another 5 minutes, stirring to prevent sticking, then add the vinegar, garlic, wine, salt, and pepper. Simmer for 15 to 20 minutes to reduce and thicken the vinaigrette.

Serve warm over just-warm or room-temperature asparagus spears.

Serves 6

Curried Shrimp and Potato Soup

I bet fresh corn off the cob would be good in this soup, and sometime you probably should try substituting rice for the potatoes used here. The shrimp dish that inspired this curried soup was always served over rice, and that certainly worked well.

¼ cup (½ stick) unsalted butter
1 cup finely chopped tart apple
1 cup finely chopped celery
3 cups finely chopped onions
3 cups water
1 pint light cream, or half-and-half

5 tablespoons curry powder
2 teaspoons salt
½ teaspoon finely ground black pepper
2 cups Fish Stock (page 3), heated
2 cups rich Chicken Stock (page 74), heated
1 pound cooked and peeled medium shrimp, each
  cut in half
1 pound white potatoes, peeled, cut into ½-inch
  dice

Garnish
  Snipped fresh chives

Melt the butter in a deep skillet and sauté the apple, celery, and onions until wilted and the onions are turning golden, about 5 minutes. Add the water and bring to a simmer. Continue simmering until almost all the water has evaporated, about 10 minutes. Purée the mixture in a food processor until smooth.

Return mixture to the skillet and whisk in the cream, curry powder, salt, and pepper. Simmer over very low heat, whisking regularly, until reduced and thickened, about 10 minutes. Stir in the fish and chicken stocks. Mix thoroughly, add the shrimp, and simmer for a few minutes.

Meanwhile, cover the diced potatoes with well-salted water and bring to a boil. Boil slowly for 5 minutes, then drain and add to the soup. Continue to simmer the soup for another 2 or 3 minutes.

Garnish each serving with chives.

Serves 6

Skillet Pepper Bread

2 cups all-purpose flour
1 teaspoon baking soda
1 teaspoon salt
¾ teaspoon finely ground black pepper
1 cup milk, approximately
  Several tablespoons slightly softened unsalted
  butter

Sift the flour, baking soda, salt, and black pepper into a large bowl. Stir in ¾ cup of the milk. Mix well; you want to wind up with a stiff dough, so add the balance of the milk a little at the time. Use it all or just a portion of it.

Heat an ungreased iron skillet or a griddle.

Pinch off walnut-size pieces of dough and roll them out until thin on a floured surface. Spread the center of each rolled-out circle with butter. Fold circle over and roll out thin again.

Test the skillet or griddle by sprinkling it with a few pinches of flour. If the flour immediately begins to brown, it is ready. Add circles of dough, allowing room to turn them. Keep turning until the dough puffs and browns. These will brown unevenly. Serve hot.

Makes 16 to 18 breads

Peppermint Pears with Pecan–Brown Sugar Shortbread

Texture is very important here, so avoid mealy pears. The cookies are a delectable version of an old standby.

> ¾ cup sugar
> ¾ cup water
> ½ lemon, cut into several pieces
> 6 medium pears (preferably Anjou), cored, peeled, and halved
> 4 or 5 large sprigs peppermint, tied

Garnish
> Mint sprigs
> Crème fraîche or yogurt sprinkled with cinnamon

Combine sugar and water in a saucepan and bring to a boil. Drop in lemon pieces and simmer for about 5 minutes. Add pears and simmer until tender but not mushy.

Remove the pears with a slotted spoon, place in a bowl, and bury the mint bundle among them. Pour syrup over all and allow to cool. Refrigerate.

To serve, discard mint and garnish pears with a sprig of fresh mint and a dollop of crème fraîche or yogurt sprinkled with cinnamon, if desired, or serve plain in the syrup with a wedge of shortbread (recipe follows).

Serves 6

PECAN–BROWN SUGAR SHORTBREAD

> 1 cup (2 sticks) unsalted butter, softened
> 1 cup light brown sugar, tightly packed
> 1 teaspoon vanilla extract
> 1 cup finely chopped pecans
> 1¼ cups all-purpose flour

Preheat oven to 325 degrees. Butter well a 9-inch round cake pan.

Beat the butter and brown sugar until fluffy. Beat in the vanilla.

Combine the pecans and flour. Add them to the butter–brown sugar mixture in 4 portions, mixing well after each addition.

Pat the mixture into the pan and pierce the top with the tines of a fork. Bake until slightly browned and puffy, about 30 minutes.

Carefully cut into wedges before allowing to cool.

Makes 16 wedges

Here's How

You can definitely make the vinaigrette, which rewarms well, a day ahead; ditto the pears and shortbread. And although I have made the soup and rewarmed it before, rewarming the shrimp does seem to toughen them a bit. Frankly, I am not sure if this small drawback outweighs the advantage of getting this done and out of the way in advance. The flavor is marvelous either way.

Asparagus can be steamed to crisp-tender in the late afternoon. Wrap them in a few damp paper towels (and a little plastic wrap) and refrigerate. Since they will be dressed with a warm vinaigrette, it is best to have the asparagus come back to room temperature before serving.

This leaves only the skillet bread to be concerned about. It is best eaten pretty soon after it has been cooked, but it can be done before the guests arrive.

Fish Soup
Dinner

Opposite: The Fish Soup dinner, including Toasted Saltines and Parmesan Toast.
Above: Vegetable Terrine. Below: Bellini Sorbet.

Fish Soup Dinner

There are plenty of ways to make fish soup, but if you start with a flavorful fish stock you can go in almost any direction you like. This soup is surprisingly light, and to continue—or rather, begin—the theme, the vegetable terrine makes a light first course.

And finishing off with peach-champagne sorbet brings the meal to a perfect close.

Menu

Vegetable Terrine with Watercress Mayonnaise
FISH SOUP
Toasted Saltines and Parmesan Toast
Bellini Sorbet
Wine
Coffee

Vegetable Terrine with Watercress Mayonnaise

This seems like a long and complicated recipe, but don't let that daunt you if you like vegetable terrines.

  2 pounds ham hocks or meaty smoked pork neck bones
  3 quarts water
  1 large carrot, broken into several pieces
  1 large onion, quartered
    Several ribs celery, broken into large pieces
  2 bay leaves
  2 carrots, peeled and cut into julienne strips
  4 medium leeks, well washed with tough outer layers removed
  2 medium potatoes, peeled and cut into thick sticks
  ¼ pound green beans, tips and stems removed
  1 large yellow or red bell pepper, roasted, peeled, and seeded
  4 envelopes unflavored gelatin
    Salt to taste
  ¼ teaspoon freshly ground black pepper
  2 egg whites, lightly beaten
  2 egg shells
    Several dashes Tabasco
  1 tablespoon cognac
    Strips of ¼-inch-thick cooked ham (optional)

Cover the ham hocks or neck bones with the water and bring to a boil. Turn down to simmer and add the carrot, onion, celery, and bay leaves. Allow to slowly boil, uncovered, for several hours. Strain out the bones and either discard the meat or reserve it to make a sandwich spread. Discard vegetables and bay leaves. Refrigerate liquid if you have time, then remove congealed fat from the top; otherwise, carefully skim fat off.

To assemble the terrine, select a 4- to 6-cup loaf pan and refrigerate. Meanwhile, separately cook all the vegetables except the peppers in the skimmed liquid until tender, being careful not to cook the potatoes so much that they fall apart. Cut the leeks in lengthwise strips after cooking. Refresh all vegetables in cold water, dry them, and refrigerate. Strain the liquid once more and measure out 4 cups. (This is likely to be about what you have.) If you don't have enough liquid, make up the difference with a little chicken stock or water. Place liquid in a saucepan and sprinkle the gelatin over it. When gelatin has softened, add salt, pepper, egg whites, and egg shells. Place saucepan over medium heat and bring to a boil, stirring all the while. Off the heat, add Tabasco and cognac. Line a strainer with a double layer of dampened cheesecloth. Pour liquid through, then discard cloth and particles. Allow gelatin to cool slightly.

Pour a thin layer of gelatin in the bottom of the cold loaf pan. Allow to set for a few minutes, then put a layer of one of the vegetables neatly over it. Cover this vegetable layer with more gelatin mixture and allow gelatin to set for a few minutes in the refrigerator before proceeding. Continue with layers of each vegetable and the ham, if you are using it, repeating the thin gelatin layer over each. When complete, cover all with gelatin up to the top of the pan. Refrigerate, covered, until set.

To serve, set in a pan of hot water just long enough to loosen the sides. Invert onto a serving platter, then chill to reset gelatin before slicing, 30 to 45 minutes.

Serve with Watercress Mayonnaise (recipe follows).

Serves 6

WATERCRESS MAYONNAISE

  ½ large bunch watercress, leaves only
  1 shallot, coarsely chopped
  2 tablespoons tarragon vinegar
  ½ teaspoon salt
    Pinch of black pepper
    Pinch of cayenne (ground red) pepper
  1 cup Homemade Mayonnaise (page 6)

Place all ingredients except mayonnaise in a food processor. Purée, scraping down sides often. Add mayonnaise and mix until just blended.

Makes 1 generous cup

Fish Soup

I really don't like this as well when made with an oily fish, so keep to fish with white flesh.

  2 tablespoons (¼ stick) unsalted butter
  2 tablespoons olive oil
  ¾ pound fennel, cleaned and sliced into ¾-inch pieces
  1 pound onions, coarsely sliced
  2 carrots, scraped and cut into coarse rings
  2 large ribs celery, cut into thick slices
  1 very large garlic clove, minced
  2 quarts rich Fish Stock (page 3), heated
  1 tablespoon fresh lemon juice
  1 teaspoon dried thyme
  1 large bay leaf
  2 cups peeled, diced potatoes
  1 pound tomatoes, peeled, seeded, and coarsely chopped
  3 sprigs fresh marjoram, tied
  1 pound firm-fleshed white fish fillets (such as tilefish), cut into 1-inch cubes
    Salt and pepper to taste

Heat butter and oil in a soup pot and sauté fennel, onions, carrots, and celery until wilted, about 5 minutes. Stir in garlic, fish stock, lemon juice, thyme, bay leaf, and potatoes. Simmer for 10 minutes, skimming foam as necessary.

   Add tomatoes, marjoram, and fish. Simmer until fish is done, another 8 to 10 minutes. Do not overcook. Remove marjoram sprigs, add salt and pepper to taste, and serve.

Serves 6 to 8

Toasted Saltines and Parmesan Toast

To my way of thinking, toasting vastly improves the taste of ordinary saltine crackers. Simply brush each cracker generously with melted butter, place on a cookie sheet, and bake in a preheated 350 degree oven until the crackers are golden, 5 minutes or so.

To make Parmesan Toast, lightly toast slices of ordinary dense white bread on both sides, either in the oven or in a toaster. Generously butter one side of each and sprinkle well with freshly grated Parmesan cheese. Return toasts to the oven to bake until golden or run under the broiler.

Bellini Sorbet

This sorbet was inspired by the Bellini cocktail made famous at Harry's Bar in Venice. It melts pretty fast, so serve it in chilled bowls.

  ¾ cup sugar
  ½ cup water
  2 pounds ripe peaches, peeled and pitted
  1 tablespoon fresh lemon juice
  1 tablespoon crème de cassis liqueur
1½ cups dry Champagne

Mix sugar and water in a saucepan. Bring to a slow simmer, stirring. When the sugar melts in a few minutes, remove from heat and allow to cool.

   Meanwhile, purée the peaches with the lemon juice in a food processor. Mix with the cooled simple syrup. Stir in cassis and Champagne.

   Place mixture in an electric ice-cream freezer, and process according to manufacturer's directions. Or place mixture in a shallow metal pan in the freezer, stirring occasionally as the mixture freezes.

Makes approximately 1 quart

Here's How

Obviously, you should make the vegetable terrine in advance. As I've said, it is time-consuming mainly because of the waiting periods required, not because this vegetable terrine is so laborious to prepare. The sauce is probably best if put together a few hours before it is to be used.

   On the day before, prepare the sorbet. Also make the soup up to the point at which the tomatoes and fish are added. Since the soup will then require only about 8 to 10 minutes of additional cooking once it is reheated, you won't have to spend too much time in the kitchen before dinner.

   As for the crackers and toast, you may as well finish them while the soup is in its final simmering, so that they will be fresh and crisp. However, you could also do this just before guests arrive and, after cooling, store them in an airtight tin.

Above: The meal by the pool. Hush Puppies are in the middle of the table. Right: Tomato Soufflé. Center: Strawberry-Apple Crumble. Far right: Green Pea and Ham Soup.

Green Pea and Ham Soup Dinner

I am really mad about fresh green peas. They must remind me of my childhood, or something. Incidentally, when I serve steamed fresh peas for a large group, I always wait until the guests arrive to shell the peas so I can get some help. This invariably works. Thank heaven it does; shelling peas is not my favorite pastime. But with four or five people shelling, it is finished in a few minutes.

To begin this green pea soup dinner, there is a tomato soufflé, a golden pinkish-orange concoction that is easy to make as soufflés go and tastes as good as it looks.

Then there are hush puppies to have along with the soup and a scrumptious and uncomplicated strawberry-apple crumble for dessert.

Menu

Tomato Soufflé
GREEN PEA AND HAM SOUP
Hush Puppies
Strawberry-Apple Crumble
Wine
Coffee

Green Pea and Ham Soup Dinner

Tomato Soufflé

I think it is best to make the tomato essence for this in advance, so you can be relaxed about the soufflé. And I only make it when tomatoes are at their peak of flavor. However, if the soufflé essence doesn't taste tomatoey enough, you could stir in a little extra good-quality tomato paste to give it a lift.

    Grated Parmesan cheese to dust inside of
        soufflé dish
  3 tablespoons chopped shallots
  5 tablespoons unsalted butter
1½ tablespoons minced garlic
  2 tablespoons chopped fresh tarragon
  ¼ cup all-purpose flour
  1 teaspoon salt
  ½ teaspoon black pepper
  2 cups peeled, seeded, and coarsely chopped
        vine-ripened tomatoes
  2 tablespoons tomato paste
  4 egg yolks, lightly beaten
  5 egg whites
  ¼ teaspoon salt
  ¼ teaspoon cream of tartar

Preheat oven to 350 degrees. Generously butter a 6- to 8-cup medium to shallow soufflé dish. Dust with finely grated Parmesan cheese and set aside.

Sauté the shallots in the butter over medium heat until wilted, about 5 minutes. Add the garlic and tarragon, then cook another few minutes more. Sprinkle with flour and cook for a few minutes, until well blended. Add salt, pepper, and tomatoes. The mixture will lump up, but keep stirring and mashing until the tomatoes begin to give up their water and a thick paste is formed. Stir in tomato paste, then add egg yolks and cook a few more minutes. Set aside.

Beat the egg whites until foamy, then add the salt and cream of tartar. Beat until stiff. Pile whites on top of the tomato mixture and fold in with an over-and-under motion until lightly mixed. Do not overmix; there can be a few streaks or lumps of white in the mixture when you pour it into the prepared dish. Place soufflé dish in a larger pan and surround with hot water. Bake until set, about 35 to 40 minutes. Serve immediately.

Serves 6

Green Pea and Ham Soup

Like most of my other soups, this one is pretty thick, but if you like a thinner soup, add more chicken stock and check the seasoning.

If you decide to make this in the winter with frozen peas (which are surprisingly good in a soup), put them into the soup unthawed and cook them just long enough to warm them through, a couple of minutes at most.

  1 tablespoon olive oil
  2 tablespoons (¼ stick) unsalted butter
  ¼ pound ham steak (½ inch thick), trimmed and
        finely diced
  ⅓ cup finely chopped celery
  ⅓ cup finely chopped carrots
  1 cup finely chopped onions
  ½ pound fresh button mushrooms, sliced
  1 small garlic clove, minced
  4 cups Chicken Stock (page 74), heated
  1 teaspoon salt
  ½ teaspoon paprika
  ¼ teaspoon finely ground black pepper
  ½ head Boston lettuce (about ¼ pound), carefully
        washed and shredded
  2 cups shelled green peas

Heat olive oil and butter in a deep saucepan and add the diced ham. Fry over medium heat until ham begins to crisp. Remove, drain, and reserve.

Add celery, carrots, and onions, and sauté until the vegetables wilt and begin to turn golden, about 3 minutes. Add the mushrooms and continue cooking for another 2 minutes, tossing all the while. Stir in the garlic, then add the chicken stock, salt, paprika, and pepper.

Add lettuce and peas to the soup. Bring to a boil and then reduce heat to a simmer. Cook for 10 minutes and turn off the heat. Stir in reserved ham and allow to sit for 15 minutes before serving.

Serves 6

Hush Puppies

Hush puppies, or at least cornbread, and green peas just seem made for one another. I always think of the two together. However, if you don't have the same fix, the Toasted Saltines on page 39 are a good substitute and couldn't be simpler.

1 cup white cornmeal
¾ teaspoon salt
1 teaspoon baking powder
¼ cup finely chopped green onions, including some tops
½ cup boiling water
1 egg, well beaten
Fat for deep-frying

Thoroughly mix cornmeal, salt, and baking powder in a large bowl. Mix in green onions. Pour in boiling water, stirring well. Stir in egg.

Heat oil in a deep pot to hot but not smoking. Drop batter by generous teaspoonfuls into hot oil and fry until golden brown. Drain on paper towels.

Makes approximately 18 hush puppies

Variation: Another version of this recipe can be made by simply mixing cornmeal, salt, and green onions, pouring hot water over all, and leaving out the egg.

Put about 1 inch of oil in a skillet, heat to very hot, and drop batter in by teaspoonfuls. Turn once and fry until brown. Drain on paper towels.

Strawberry-Apple Crumble

Strawberries and apples seem to have an affinity for one another. It's a wonder they aren't combined more often. The coconut is there for the crunch.

½ cup dried tart cherries (optional)
¼ cup dark rum (optional)
4 Granny Smith apples, cored, peeled, and cut into thin slices
2 pints strawberries, hulled and cut in half
3 tablespoons fresh lemon juice
½ cup canned shredded unsweetened coconut
½ cup sugar
½ cup all-purpose flour
½ teaspoon ground cinnamon
½ cup (2 sticks) unsalted butter
   Vanilla ice cream or sweetened whipped cream

Preheat oven to 350 degrees.

If you are using them, place cherries in a shallow bowl and toss with rum. Allow to marinate for at least 30 minutes. Drain cherries and reserve rum.

Butter a shallow oval baking dish and arrange apple slices over the bottom. Sprinkle the cherries over the apples. Top with the berries and sprinkle with the lemon juice.

Place coconut, sugar, flour, and cinnamon in a bowl and mix well. Cut butter into bits and mix with the coconut mixture, using your hands. Mixture should be crumbly. Spread evenly over the fruit and press down lightly. Bake until lightly browned, about 30 minutes.

Serve hot or at room temperature with vanilla ice cream or sweetened whipped cream to which you have added a bit of the reserved rum.

Serves 6

Here's How

The day before you can prepare the soup up to the point of adding the lettuce and peas, as well as make the tomato essence for the soufflé.

Since the soup needs to be served just warm, when you are about ready to serve, bring it to a simmer and add the lettuce and peas. Cook for a minute and turn off the heat. It can wait until you whip up, literally, and bake the soufflé.

While the soufflé is baking, measure the ingredients for the hush puppies and put the oil in its pot. Turn on low heat under the kettle of water. All of this is so that after you finish eating the soufflé, you can quickly make the hush puppies. If this sounds too hurried, make the hush puppies while the soufflé is baking, and put them in a warming oven while you finish your first course. It's not as good as the other way, but better than no hush puppies at all.

I'd prepare the dessert to come out of the oven about the time when guests are due to arrive.

Okra Chowder Dinner

It seems I'm always trying to get people who have never had it (or think they don't like it) to try okra. So here I go again. Okra combines naturally with corn and tomatoes, so of course it makes a delightful chowder.

And the dessert is made with blackberries, which often are in season about the same time as okra. It's all very down-home.

To start the meal is grilled tuna brochette, simple and satisfying. Don't let people eat too much because they won't have room for the rest of the dinner. Tuna is filling.

Menu

Tuna en Brochette
OKRA CHOWDER
Green Peppercorn Mustard Rolls
Blackberry Buckle with Blackberry Sauce
Wine
Coffee

Opposite page, counterclockwise from top: Green Peppercorn Mustard Rolls rising, the baked rolls, Blackberry Buckle, Tuna en Brochette on the grill, the brochettes marinating. This page: Okra Chowder.

Okra Chowder Dinner

Tuna en Brochette

  1½ pounds tuna steaks (½ inch thick), cut into 1-inch
      cubes
   2 red onions, peeled, quartered, and separated
   ½ cup balsamic vinegar
   ½ cup safflower oil
   1 very large garlic clove, minced
   2 large bay leaves, crumbled
     Salt and pepper
     Lemon slices

Alternate cubes of tuna with pieces of red onion on 6
pairs of wooden skewers. Place in a shallow pan. Whisk
together the vinegar and oil, and pour over fish. Sprinkle with garlic and bay leaves. Allow to marinate for 1
hour, turning several times. Drain the marinade and reserve.

    Salt and pepper the skewers before grilling them over
charcoal (or under the broiler) for approximately 3 minutes per side or until done. Do not overcook.

    Heat the reserved marinade in a small saucepan and
simmer for a minute before straining. Serve individual
pieces of tuna and onion with a slice of lemon and spoon
some of the heated marinade over each.

Serves 6 to 8

Variation: You can also serve the tuna with a dollop of
"marinade mayonnaise." To make this, remove several
tablespoons of the marinade before pouring it over the
fish and reduce for a minute over medium to low heat.
Allow to cool, then stir this essence into a cup of Homemade Mayonnaise (page 6) along with a teaspoon of
very finely chopped parsley.

Okra Chowder

*If you don't have time to find the pancetta, substitute a
good smoked bacon, preferably not sugar cured. Blanch it
before using.*
   *Should you want to have this chowder in winter, both
okra and corn freeze tolerably well.*

   ¼ pound pancetta (Italian unsmoked bacon) in 1
      piece, cut into medium dice
   2 tablespoons (¼ stick) unsalted butter
   ¼ cup safflower oil
   1 large onion, coarsely chopped
   2 medium shallots, finely chopped
   1 pound fresh okra, tops and tips removed, cut into
      ½-inch slices
   1 (14½-ounce) can peeled tomatoes (no paste),
      drained and coarsely chopped
   7 cups Chicken Stock (page 74)
   1 teaspoon salt
     Scant ½ teaspoon dried thyme
   2 medium baking potatoes (about 1¼ pounds),
      peeled and coarsely diced
   2 large ears yellow corn, kernels cut from the cob
      and with milk scraped out

Bring a saucepan of water to a boil and blanch the pancetta for 2 minutes. Drain and set aside.

    Place butter and safflower oil in a deep pot and when
hot, add the pancetta. Brown the pieces and reserve.
Add onion, shallots, and okra. Cook over medium heat
until onion begins to brown. Add tomatoes and cook another 5 minutes, stirring. Add stock, salt, and thyme.
Simmer, skimming any foam, for 10 minutes.

    Add potatoes and slowly boil for 10 minutes, skim-
ming (oil will have started to rise to the surface). Add
corn kernels, corn milk, and pancetta. Simmer for an
additional 2 minutes, then turn off the heat. Allow to
rest on the stove for 15 minutes before serving.

Serves 6 to 8

Green Peppercorn Mustard Rolls

*The hint of green peppercorn mustard gives these rolls a
nice snap. They are good with any hearty flavored soup.*

   1 package active dry yeast
   1 teaspoon sugar
   1 cup warm water (105°–115°F)
  ⅔ cup green peppercorn mustard
   4 cups all-purpose flour
  1½ teaspoons salt
     Melted butter

Place yeast and sugar in a small bowl with the water. When dissolved, stir in mustard and 1 cup of the flour to make a paste. Mix well. Add the rest of the flour and salt, mixing as you go. Turn out onto a floured surface and knead dough until smooth and elastic, approximately 7 minutes.

Grease a large crockery bowl and place the dough in it; cover with a tea towel. Allow dough to rise in a warm, draft-free spot until at least doubled in bulk, about 1 hour.

Punch the dough down and form it into 18 round balls. Place them on a greased cookie sheet and allow to rise once again, covered, until doubled in size.

Meanwhile preheat the oven to 350 degrees. Bake the rolls until golden, approximately 20 minutes. The rolls can be brushed with melted butter during the last few minutes of baking to make them browner.

Makes 18 rolls

Blackberry Buckle with Blackberry Sauce

This is a Southern variation on a New England favorite.

  2 cups plus 2 tablespoons all-purpose flour
  2 teaspoons baking powder
  ½ teaspoon salt
  ¼ cup (½ stick) unsalted butter, softened
  ¾ cup sugar
  1 large egg
  ½ cup milk
  1 generous pint fresh blackberries
    Whipped cream flavored with blackberry brandy
    or rum

Topping
  ¼ cup (½ stick) unsalted butter, softened
  ½ cup sugar
  ⅓ cup all-purpose flour
  ½ teaspoon ground cinnamon

Preheat the oven to 375 degrees. Grease an 8-inch round springform pan. Set aside.

Sift together 2 cups of the flour, baking powder, and salt. Set aside. Cream the butter and sugar until fluffy, about 3 minutes. Beat in the egg, then add the flour mixture in 3 parts, alternating with the milk. Toss the berries with the remaining 2 tablespoons of flour (to separate and scatter them evenly through the dough) and fold in. Pour batter into the prepared pan.

Combine the ingredients for the topping with a fork to make a crumbly mixture. Sprinkle this over the batter.

Bake for 1 hour. If a cake tester does not come out clean, bake for another 5 to 10 minutes.

Let cake cool; run a knife around edges and release sides of the pan. Serve with Blackberry Sauce (recipe follows) and generously spiked whipped cream.

Serves 6 to 8

BLACKBERRY SAUCE

  1 cup fresh blackberries
  6 tablespoons superfine sugar
  1 tablespoon lemon juice
  1 tablespoon crème de cassis (or blackberry liqueur)

Sprinkle berries with sugar and refrigerate for about 1 hour. Purée in a food processor, with lemon juice and cassis.

Makes about 1½ cups

Here's How

Make the dough for the rolls and keep it in the refrigerator so you can bake them as you need them. The dough will remain fresh for about a week if tightly covered.

The soup can be made a day in advance up to the point of adding the potatoes and corn. About 30 minutes before serving, bring the soup to a boil and add the potatoes and corn. Cook for about 10 minutes and turn off the heat.

Make the cake a day ahead if you like. The tuna is best eaten just after it is cooked, but it is still good when it cools. So the only real timing you need to concern yourself with is with baking the rolls and finishing the soup.

I was brought up on all sorts of greens, and even today they remain one of my preferred vegetables, with mustard greens and turnip greens topping the list. They are not often used in soups, which is too bad because aside from being so tasty, they are filled with vitamins.

This is fairly hearty, so it is best for a meal late in the season when the warmest weather has passed.

To begin, there is a terrific pasta dish with which you might want to serve the rye breadsticks (serve them with the soup as well). And round it all out with a cassis sorbet and a couple of lemon cookies.

Menu

Fettuccine with Four Cheeses
GREENS, TURNIP, AND
CORN SOUP
Rye Breadsticks
Cassis Sorbet with Lemon Kisses
Wine
Coffee

<u>Top</u>: *Fettuccine with Four Cheeses.* <u>Left</u>: *Cassis Sorbet with Lemon Kisses.* <u>Opposite</u>: *Greens, Turnip, and Corn Soup.*

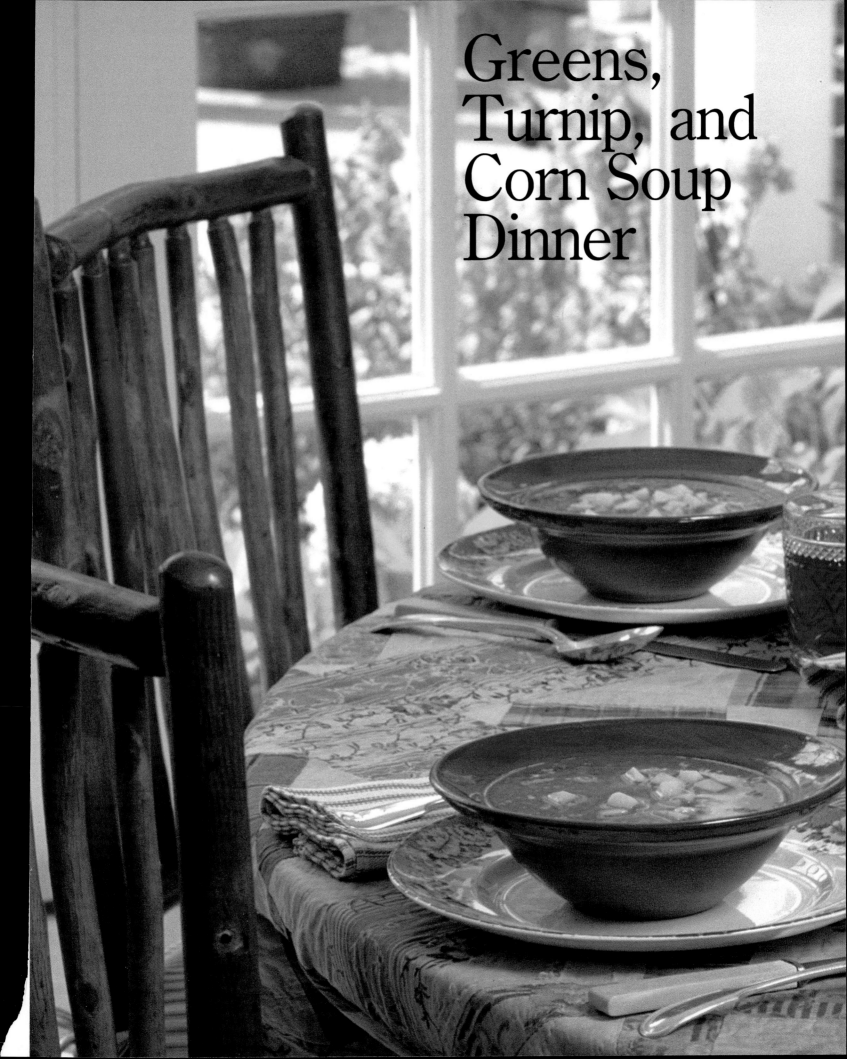

Greens, Turnip, and Corn Soup Dinner

Greens, Turnip, and Corn Soup Dinner

Fettuccine with Four Cheeses

The secret to the preparation of this tasty pasta dish is to have everything heated, chopped, drained, etc., ready to go when you assemble it. Do it all quickly.

If you like, you might also add chopped prosciutto. As a matter of fact, by adding ham and steamed fresh green peas to this dish you have the makings of a quick and easy Sunday supper. All you need then is a salad and a bit of fruit for dessert.

> ½ cup minced onion
> 1 tablespoon minced garlic
> ¼ cup (½ stick) unsalted butter
> 1 cup ricotta cheese
> 4 ounces mild chèvre (goat cheese)
> ½ teaspoon salt
> Pinch of cayenne (ground red) pepper
> 1½ ounces freshly grated Parmesan cheese
> 1 pound fettuccine, cooked al dente and drained
> ½ cup good-quality mild olive oil, heated
> ½ pound mozzarella cheese, cut into small cubes
> 2 generous tablespoons chopped fresh chives

Sauté the onion and garlic in the butter until just wilted, 4 to 5 minutes. Stir in the ricotta and chèvre. Allow to heat and melt over low heat, stirring. Mix in salt, cayenne, and Parmesan cheese.

Toss pasta and oil together, then add the ricotta mixture and toss again. Add the mozzarella and chives and toss quickly. You want to get the pasta served before the mozzarella has a chance to completely melt.

Serve on individual warmed plates, with additional Parmesan on the side if desired.

Serves 6

Greens, Turnip, and Corn Soup

If you don't see mustard greens around, and you are near a market that sells really fresh produce, have them ask their supplier about turnip greens. These are merely the tops of white turnips. Kale and collard greens are the other choices, but neither compares with mustard or turnip greens.

> 2 strips thick-sliced bacon
> 2 tablespoons olive oil
> 2 tablespoons (¼ stick) unsalted butter
> 2 large shallots, coarsely chopped
> 1 pound onions, peeled and coarsely chopped
> 1 rib celery, coarsely chopped
> 1 large garlic clove, minced
> 2½ pounds mustard greens
> 2 packages instant chicken stock, approximately .19 ounces each
> 2 teaspoons salt
> 1 teaspoon black pepper
> ½ teaspoon dried thyme
> 6 cups rich Chicken Stock (page 74)
> 2 teaspoons lemon juice
> ¼ teaspoon Tabasco
> 1¼ pounds young white turnips, peeled and cubed
> 6 large ears corn, kernels cut from the cob and cobs scraped for milk

Garnish
> Chopped fresh chives
> Lemon slice

In a deep pot, fry bacon until crisp. Set aside. Reserve 1 tablespoon fat. Add olive oil and butter. Sauté shallots, onions, and celery until lightly browned, about 5 minutes. Add garlic.

Carefully wash greens and remove tough stems. Tear into large pieces and place in pot with only the water clinging to them. Sprinkle with instant chicken stock, salt, pepper, and thyme. Cover tightly and cook over medium heat until greens are wilted and tender, about 10 minutes.

Transfer to a food processor and purée. Return to soup pot and add chicken stock, lemon juice, and Tabasco. Bring to a slow boil and add turnips. Simmer until they start to become tender, about 10 minutes.

Add corn kernels and milk. Continue cooking for another 5 minutes. Correct seasoning, turn off heat, and let sit, uncovered, for 15 to 20 minutes before serving. Garnish with chopped chives or a thin slice of lemon.

Serves 6

Rye Breadsticks

Breadsticks are a bit time-consuming to make, but these are really good. However, you can substitute a nice crusty loaf of French or Italian bread.

¼ cup dark molasses
1½ teaspoons salt
1 tablespoon unsalted butter, melted
½ cup boiling water
2 tablespoons caraway seeds
¾ cup warm water (105°–115°F)
1 package active dry yeast
2 cups rye flour
1¾ cups all-purpose flour
1 egg white
2 tablespoons water
Additional caraway seeds and kosher (coarse) salt

In a small bowl, combine the molasses, salt, melted butter, boiling water, and caraway seeds. Set aside.

Place warm water in a small bowl and sprinkle in the yeast. When yeast is dissolved and the molasses mixture is just warm, mix the two together. Pour into a large bowl and add the rye flour. Stir to mix thoroughly. Turn out onto a floured surface and knead in the flour. Continue to knead until dough is glossy and elastic, about 5 to 7 minutes.

Place dough in an oiled bowl, cover with a tea towel, and allow to rise to double its bulk in a warm, draft-free place; it should take about 1 hour. Punch down and divide dough into 20 balls of equal size. Roll each ball into a stick and place on greased cookie sheets. Allow to rise until doubled in size, about 30 to 45 minutes.

Meanwhile, preheat oven to 400 degrees.

Combine egg white and water. Brush on each stick and sprinkle with caraway seeds and kosher salt.

Bake for approximately 20 minutes, or longer if you like them dry.

Makes 20 sticks

Cassis Sorbet with Lemon Kisses

The cookies are the invention of my friend Tom Byrne. They are meltingly good.

2½ cups water
1½ cups sugar
¾ cup crème de cassis (black currant liqueur)
3 tablespoons fresh lemon juice
2 tablespoons grated lemon zest

Stir water and sugar together in a saucepan over medium heat until sugar dissolves. Set aside to cool. Add cassis, lemon juice, and lemon zest. Mix and chill. Pour into an ice-cream maker and freeze according to manufacturer's directions.

Serve in chilled bowls with Lemon Kisses (recipe follows).

Makes approximately 1½ pints

LEMON KISSES

½ cup (1 stick) unsalted butter, softened
¾ cup sifted confectioners' sugar
1 large egg yolk
Juice of 1 lemon
Zest of 1 lemon
½ teaspoon vanilla extract
1½ cups all-purpose flour

Topping
Zest of 1 lemon mixed with ¼ cup sugar

Preheat oven to 350 degrees. Lightly grease a cookie sheet.

Cream the butter and confectioners' sugar until fluffy, about 5 minutes. Mix in yolk thoroughly, then add lemon juice and zest and vanilla. Mix in flour in 4 portions. Stir well.

Drop by the tablespoonful onto cookie sheet. Top each with a light sprinkling of the lemon zest and sugar.

Bake until lightly browned, approximately 12 minutes. Cool on a rack.

Makes approximately 24 cookies

Here's How

Make the soup, breadsticks, sorbet, and cookies the day before. This means you only have to cope with the pasta course, an easy chore that requires almost more organizing than cooking.

Reheat the soup by simply letting it simmer for about a minute before turning off the heat. Do this just as you are putting the pasta in to boil, and the soup will be the right temperature after you finish the pasta course.

Clockwise from upper left: Carrot and Dill Soup;
Roasted Tomato, Rice, and Scallop Soup; Sweet
Potato Vichyssoise; Pimiento Soup.

VARIATIONS ON SUMMER SOUP MEALS

Soups

I hope the scrambling of courses here will encourage you to see the possibilities for creating a variety of different menus. Obviously, such a mixing will increase the number of meals you might come up with from the assortment of courses in this group of recipes.

For instance, why not serve the Corn Soufflé as an appetizer with the Tomato, Rice, and Scallop Soup and Sesame Breadsticks, finally finishing with Grapefruit Mousse?

All you need do to get the most from this is to let your imagination and personal likes and dislikes be your guide.

Carrot and Dill Soup

The combination of carrots and dill is a marriage made in heaven. Add as much dill as you like.

      2 tablespoons (¼ stick) unsalted butter
      6 ounces onion, coarsely chopped
   1¾ pounds carrots (weight after removing tops)
      ¾ pound sweet potato
      ½ pound baking potato
      5 cups rich Chicken Stock (page 74)
   1½ teaspoons salt
         Scant ½ teaspoon freshly ground white pepper
      1 tablespoon fresh lemon juice
      2 generous tablespoons finely chopped fresh dill
         Sour cream, crème fraîche, or yogurt

Preheat oven to 400 degrees.

Melt butter in a medium skillet and sauté onion until light golden and just beginning to brown.

Carefully scrub carrots and cut into rings, unpeeled. Steam until soft.

Meanwhile, place sweet and white potatoes in oven and bake until soft, about 1 hour.

Scrape sautéed onion into a food processor, deglaze pan with a little of the chicken stock, and add this to the onion. Add carrots and purée. Scoop out potato pulp and add to processor along with salt, white pepper, and lemon juice. Purée until thoroughly mixed and very fine. Pour mixture into a saucepan, then add dill and stock. Simmer over very low heat for about 15 minutes.

Soup may be thinned with additional stock, milk, or cream. Correct seasoning, and serve warm with a dollop of sour cream, yogurt, or crème fraîche on top.

Serves 6 to 8

Pimiento Soup

To tell you the truth, I am a sucker for almost anything that has roasted red peppers in it. Must be all that Cajun food I was brought up on, where almost every dish started by sautéeing onions, celery, and green peppers.

Serve this soup just a little bit chilled, maybe with an additional very light sprinkling of white pepper on top of the crème fraîche. It may also need a bit more salt if the soup is very cold.

   3½ pounds ripe tomatoes
      2 large red bell peppers
   1½ tablespoons unsalted butter
      ¾ pound onions, coarsely chopped
      1 small garlic clove, minced
      1 small rib celery, coarsely chopped
      1 medium carrot, coarsely grated
      6 cups rich Chicken Stock (page 74)
         Salt and pepper to taste
         Sour cream or crème fraîche

Put tomatoes in a foil-lined shallow baking pan and set under the broiler. Roast them as you would peppers, turning with tongs until the skin blackens, about 10 minutes. Remove tomatoes to a plate and set aside. They will give up quite a bit of liquid by the time you are ready to use them; drain it off and discard.

Roast the red peppers as you did the tomatoes. When the skins are blackened, put peppers in a paper bag and fold the top shut. Set aside.

Put butter, onions, garlic, celery, and carrot in a saucepan with ¼ cup of the chicken stock. Simmer, covered, over low heat for 10 minutes. Shake or stir to prevent sticking; do not allow to brown. When vegetables are soft, set aside.

Peel tomatoes and cut out stem ends. Add pulp to wilted onion mixture and simmer, covered, for 15 minutes. Stir occasionally to prevent scorching. Pour mixture into a strainer and mash the solids through to get rid of the seeds. (Giving the strained pulp a few whirls in a food processor makes this much easier.) Return strained vegetables to the saucepan and add balance of the chicken stock. Simmer for 30 minutes, uncovered. Skim as necessary.

Remove the peppers from the bag, rub off the blackened skins, and remove seeds. Purée in the food processor. Add to the tomato mixture and let simmer for just a few minutes. Let soup cool and then correct seasoning. Serve slightly chilled, with a large spoonful of sour cream or crème fraîche on top.

Serves 6 to 8

Roasted Tomato, Rice, and Scallop Soup

I think roasting tomatoes instead of just skinning them enhances their flavor—and it is easy to do.

     3½ pounds ripe tomatoes
     1½ tablespoons unsalted butter
     ¾ pound onions, coarsely chopped
      1 small rib celery, coarsely chopped
      2 very small carrots, coarsely shredded
      6 cups rich Chicken Stock (page 74)
     1½ tablespoons chopped fresh parsley plus 2 extra
           sprigs
      3 tablespoons chopped fresh chervil
      3 tablespoons long-grain white rice
           Salt and pepper to taste
      1 pound shucked bay scallops
     ½ cup dry white wine
           Small bay leaf

Put tomatoes in a foil-lined pan under the broiler and roast them as you would red peppers, turning with tongs as the skin begins to blacken. This will take about 10 minutes or so. Pick off the blackened skin. (Any skin you can't get rid of will be taken care of later.)

While tomatoes are roasting, put butter, onions, celery, and carrots in a saucepan with about 1 cup of the chicken stock. Simmer, covered, over low heat for about 10 minutes. Stir to prevent sticking and do not allow to brown. Add the tomatoes and all but ½ cup of the remaining stock. Cover again and continue simmering over low heat for another 15 minutes. Stir to prevent scorching.

When tomatoes become pulpy, purée in a food processor (in batches if necessary), then strain out seeds and skin, pushing through the solids. Return to saucepan and add chopped parsley, chervil, rice, salt, and pepper. Simmer, uncovered, for 10 minutes. Test rice for doneness and cook another few minutes if not done.

Meanwhile, place scallops, wine, remaining ½ cup stock, bay leaf, and parsley sprigs in a small saucepan. Bring rapidly to a simmer and cook until just tender, about 3 minutes if scallops are small. Remove bay leaf and parsley, and stir scallops and pan juice into the tomato soup.

Serves 6 to 8

Variation: For a good, old-fashioned tomato and rice soup, make the above recipe and eliminate the scallops and wine, but use all the stock.

Sweet Potato Vichyssoise

I'm a nut about sweet potatoes and am amazed that I never thought before now to make this variation of the classic vichyssoise.

     2½ pounds sweet potatoes (approximately)
     1¾ cups sliced green onions (mostly white parts)
      5 cups rich Chicken Stock (page 74)
           Salt to taste
           White pepper (optional)
     ½ cup heavy cream
           Chopped fresh chives

Preheat oven to 400 degrees.

Place potatoes in the oven and bake until soft, about 1 hour.

Meanwhile put green onions in a large saucepan with about 1 cup of the chicken stock. Simmer until tender, about 15 minutes.

Scoop out the cooked sweet potato pulp (you should have about 3 cups). Place pulp in a food processor along with the green onions and chicken stock in which they were cooked. Purée, then return to pot and add remaining stock. Simmer a few minutes longer. Salt to taste. You can add a little more stock if the soup is too thick and a dash of white pepper if desired. Refrigerate soup until ready to use.

To serve, stir in cream and top with chopped chives.

Serves 6 to 8

First Courses

Top: Corn Soufflé with Herb Sauce.
Center: Onion-Bacon Pie. *Bottom:* Potted Shrimp.
Right: Broiled Fennel with Pancetta.

First Courses

Potted Shrimp

Luckily this is rather filling, so the expensive shrimp go a long way.

      ¾ cup (1½ sticks) unsalted butter
      ¾ teaspoon grated nutmeg
      ¾ teaspoon ground mace
          Pinch of cayenne (ground red) pepper
      ½ teaspoon salt
    1½ pounds medium shrimp, peeled, deveined, and cut
          in half
          Toast
          Lemon wedges

Melt the butter in a medium skillet and when foamy, stir in the spices, cayenne, and salt. Add the shrimp and cook, tossing, until just pink. Do not let butter burn or brown. Remove shrimp to a small crock and pour butter mixture over all. Pack shrimp in crock, but do not crush. Refrigerate until firm. Serve with toast and lemon wedges.

Serves 6

Corn Soufflé with Herb Sauce

The thing that seems to stop most people from serving a soufflé as a first course is that it should be eaten as soon as it comes out of the oven. Well, by planning soup as the main course, the meal can be prepared almost entirely in advance, freeing you to spend a little extra effort on your first course.

    2 tablespoons (¼ stick) unsalted butter
    2 tablespoons all-purpose flour
    1 cup milk
    3 medium eggs, separated
    2 generous cups fresh corn kernels, cut from the
        cob and scraped (about 4 large ears)
    1 teaspoon sugar
    1 teaspoon salt
    ¼ teaspoon white pepper

Preheat oven to 350 degrees. Generously butter a 6-cup soufflé dish. Put a kettle of water over low heat. You will need this to surround the soufflé when it is baked.

Melt butter in a saucepan and sprinkle with the flour; cook for several minutes, stirring, until well blended. Add the milk, whisking all the while, and continue to cook until thickened, about 3 minutes. Beat the yolks with a fork and add a little of the white sauce to heat them before whisking them into the sauce. Cook for 1 minute more, whisking; off the heat, mix in all other ingredients, except the egg whites. Allow to cool slightly.

Beat the egg whites until stiff, but not dry. Fold whites into corn mixture with an over-and-under motion until well blended. Do not overmix; stir just until all white streaks have disappeared. Pour into prepared soufflé dish and place dish into a larger pan. Surround with hot water and bake until puffy and brown, about 30 to 35 minutes.

Serve immediately on a slick of Herb Sauce (recipe follows).

Serves 6

HERB SAUCE

      2 tablespoons (¼ stick) unsalted butter
      3 tablespoons minced shallots
      1 tablespoon minced garlic
      1 tablespoon chopped fresh rosemary
      2 tablespoons all-purpose flour
    2½ cups milk
      ¾ teaspoon salt
      ¼ teaspoon white pepper
          Pinch of cayenne (ground red) pepper
      3 tablespoons chopped fresh chives
      3 tablespoons chopped fresh parsley

Melt butter in a small saucepan and sauté shallots, garlic, and rosemary over medium heat until well wilted, about 5 minutes. Sprinkle flour over all, mix, and continue to cook for a few minutes. Whisk milk in slowly. Cook over medium to low heat, stirring all the while, for about 5 more minutes. Blend in salt, white pepper, cayenne, chives, and parsley. Serve warm.

Makes approximately 3 cups

Broiled Fennel with Pancetta

Cooked fennel is a fairly new enthusiasm for me. I had always just assumed that I didn't particularly care for its taste. I've mended my ways.

3 large fennel bulbs (about 1½ pounds), trimmed top and bottom, and cut lengthwise into generous ¼-inch slices
6 or more tablespoons good-quality olive oil
1 large lime
Salt
Freshly ground black pepper
¼ pound pancetta (Italian unsmoked bacon), sliced thin (see Note)
6 or more tablespoons coarsely grated Parmesan cheese

Garnish
Lime slices
1 large red bell pepper, roasted, peeled, seeded, and cut into strips
Black olives cured in oil

Preheat broiler.

Place slices of fennel in a single layer in a shallow pan. Smear generously with the olive oil, then sprinkle with the juice of half the lime. Salt and generously pepper.

Broil for 5 minutes. Some edges will blacken slightly. Carefully cover fennel completely with the pancetta and return to the broiler. Broil until pancetta is crisp, about 1½ minutes. Using flat-end tongs, turn individual slices of fennel with the pancetta so that the pancetta is on the bottom. Place under broiler for 3 more minutes. Remove and sprinkle with Parmesan cheese, making sure all surfaces are coated. Return to broiler until cheese starts to brown, about 1½ to 2 minutes.

Allow to remain in the pan until ready to serve. Do not refrigerate, but serve at room temperature.

To serve, arrange slices of fennel and pancetta on individual plates and squeeze the other lime half over all. Pour oil from the pan over each serving. (Add additional oil if there is not enough.) Additional pepper may be added also.

Garnish each with a small slice of lime, a few strips of roasted red pepper, and black olives.

Serves 6 to 8

Note: When you purchase the pancetta, have the very thin slices placed on a sheet of wax paper, not touching or overlapping. If one slice is put on top of the other without paper in between, they will stick together.

Onion-Bacon Pie

The dough recipe makes enough for 1 double-crust or 2 open-face 10-inch pies. It also freezes very well.

Pie Crust
2½ cups all-purpose flour
½ cup (1 stick) cold unsalted butter, cut into bits
⅓ cup cold solid vegetable shortening, cut into hunks
¼ teaspoon salt
⅓ cup ice water

Onion-Bacon Filling
¼ pound thick-sliced smoked bacon, cut into squares
3 tablespoons butter
2 pounds sweet onions (Vidalia, if possible), coarsely chopped
1 teaspoon minced garlic
1 tablespoon minced fresh rosemary
4 large eggs
1½ cups heavy cream
1½ teaspoons salt
¼ teaspoon black pepper

To make the pie crust, place flour, butter and shortening, and salt in a food processor. Process, switching off and on, until mixture resembles coarse meal. Add ice water and process just until mixture begins to cling together. Form into a ball and place between 2 sheets of wax paper. Flatten into a circle and chill.

Preheat oven to 425 degrees.

Roll out dough on a floured surface and line a 10-inch pie pan. Cut off excess, leaving about ½ inch all around, which will be tucked under before you crimp edges. Prick bottom in 4 or 5 places with the tines of a fork. Very carefully line the pan with foil and weight it down with a layer of dried beans or pie weights.

Bake for 10 minutes. Remove foil and beans and bake another 10 minutes, until golden. Set aside to cool.

To make filling, preheat oven to 350 degrees.

Cook the bacon in a large skillet until most of the fat has been rendered but bacon is not brown or crisp. Remove bacon with a slotted spoon and drain on paper towels. Discard fat and wipe out skillet.

Melt butter in skillet and sauté onions until well wilted but not browned, about 5 minutes. Add garlic and rosemary after onions have cooked for about 2 minutes. Mix.

To assemble pie, sprinkle bacon over cooled bottom crust and top with the onion mixture. Beat eggs until foamy, then whisk in the cream, salt, and pepper. Pour over all and bake until puffy and set, about 45 minutes.

Serves 6 as a main course or 8 as a first course

Above: Garlic Pizza Squares. *Below:* Corn Wafers.

Breads

Above: Sesame Breadsticks. *Below:* Tomato Gougère.

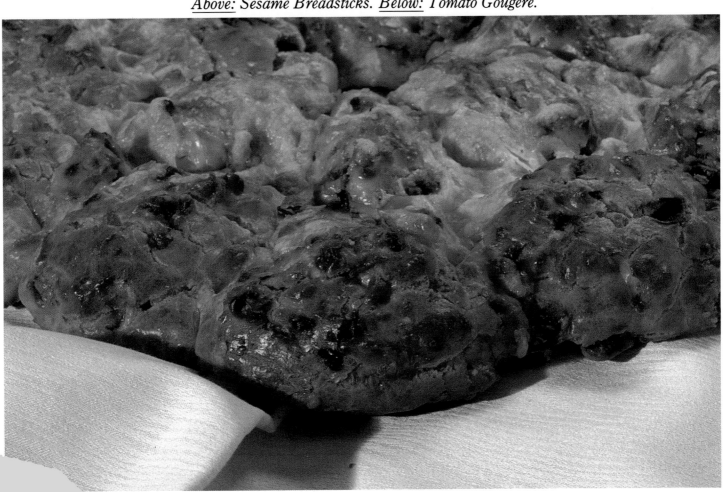

Breads

Garlic Pizza Squares

If you like garlic, this is for you.

3 envelopes active dry yeast
2 tablespoons sugar
1 cup warm water (105°–115°F)
4 cups all-purpose flour
1 tablespoon plus ½ teaspoon salt
3 tablespoons olive oil
2 tablespoons (¼ stick) unsalted butter
2 heaping tablespoons minced garlic
⅛ teaspoon black pepper

Mix yeast and sugar in a small bowl and pour warm water over. Stir and let stand until dissolved, about 10 to 15 minutes.

Mix flour and 1 tablespoon of the salt. Make a well in the center. Add 1 tablespoon of the olive oil to the yeast mixture and stir. Pour into the well and mix into a stiff dough. Knead until elastic and shiny, about 7 minutes. Place dough in an oiled crockery bowl, cover loosely with a tea towel, and allow to rise in a warm, draft-free spot until doubled in bulk, about 1 hour.

Meanwhile, mix remaining olive oil and salt, butter, garlic, and pepper in a small pan. Cook over very low heat until garlic is just softened, being careful not to brown garlic. Set aside.

When dough is ready, preheat oven to 425 degrees. Grease 2 cookie sheets.

Roll out dough until very thin, ¼ inch thick. Cut into 5-inch squares and place on cookie sheets. Paint the top of each with the garlic-oil mixture. Bake until golden, approximately 10 to 15 minutes.

Makes approximately 12 squares

Corn Wafers

These wonderful, crisp little wafers are so easy to prepare you will want to make them every time you serve soup.

You might vary them by adding a bit of prepared Cajun seasoning to the batter.

¾ cup white cornmeal
½ teaspoon salt
1 cup boiling water
2 tablespoons (¼ stick) margarine, melted
Unsalted butter

Preheat oven to 425 degrees. Grease 2 cookie sheets or coat with vegetable cooking spray.

Mix cornmeal and salt in a bowl and pour in boiling water, stirring all the while to keep lumps from forming. Stir in margarine.

Drop 1 tablespoon at the time onto the cookie sheets. This batter should be liquid enough to spread out into a 3-inch circle. If it doesn't spread, add a bit more water. Bake until golden brown around the edges and crispy, about 20 minutes. Serve with sweet butter.

Makes approximately 36 wafers.

Sesame Breadsticks

These are a bit tedious to make but are fun to do if you like to make breads. And their flavor sure beats the store-bought variety.

1½ teaspoons active dry yeast
1 cup warm water (105°–115°F)
1 teaspoon sugar
½ teaspoon salt
2½ cups all-purpose flour, approximately
   White sesame seeds
1 large egg white
1½ teaspoons water

Place yeast, warm water, and sugar in a large bowl. Mix. When yeast has dissolved, add salt and 2 cups of the flour. You want a fairly stiff dough. If mixture is still sticky, add the balance of the flour a little at a time. Turn out onto a floured surface and knead for 7 or 8 minutes, or knead in a mixer with a dough hook. Return to bowl and cover with cling wrap. Allow to triple in bulk in a warm, draft-free place; it will take several hours.

Punch down and allow to rise for another 30 minutes.

Preheat oven to 450 degrees. Generously grease 2 cookie sheets.

Divide dough into 8 parts, and roll each into a stick (about 16 to 18 inches long). If you mess up one of them, form dough into a ball and start over. Sprinkle very generously with seeds and press them in, or roll the stick in the seeds. Place breadsticks on cookie sheets and allow to rest, covered by tea towels, for 30 minutes.

Just before baking, mix egg white and water, and paint the top of each stick. (This is really optional, but will make the sticks browner.) Bake until golden, about 15 to 17 minutes.

Makes approximately 16 sticks

Tomato Gougère

Gougère, the delectable hot cheese pastry from France, makes a very impressive presentation, considering how uncomplicated it is to make.

It is also very good to serve with drinks before dinner in colder weather.

1½ cups water
½ cup (1 stick) plus 1 tablespoon unsalted butter
2 teaspoons salt
1½ cups all-purpose flour
6 eggs
2 cups grated Emmental cheese
1 cup coarsely chopped drained sun-dried tomatoes

Preheat oven to 400 degrees. Grease a cookie sheet.

Bring water to boil in a medium saucepan and add the butter. When melted, add salt and flour, all at once. Stir over low heat for a few minutes until the mixture makes a ball and pulls away from the sides of the pan. Off the heat, beat in the eggs one at a time, mixing well after each addition. Reserve about ½ cup of the cheese and mix the balance, along with the tomatoes, into the dough.

Using heaping tablespoonfuls, make a circle of dough on the cookie sheet, leaving a 2-inch space in the middle. Keep adding tablespoonfuls of dough to the outside of the circle (with each spoonful touching the ones next to it) until all the dough is used. Sprinkle reserved cheese over all.

Bake until golden and puffy, about 35 to 40 minutes. Serve warm, pull apart to eat.

Serves 6 to 8

Desserts

Opposite: Hazelnut Meringue Cookies with Mixed Fruit. Left: Gingered Peaches with Pecan Tiles. Below: Melon Balls with Cherries. Bottom: Grapefruit Mousse with Crushed Raspberries.

Desserts

Grapefruit Mousse with Crushed Raspberries

Here is a delicious and easy mousse.

    1 envelope unflavored gelatin
    ¼ cup cold water
    ¾ cup frozen grapefruit juice concentrate (pink, if
        possible), thawed but not diluted
    ¾ cup sugar
      Pinch of salt
    2 tablespoons lemon juice
    1 teaspoon grated lemon rind
    2 cups heavy cream, whipped
    1 pint raspberries

In a ceramic or glass bowl, sprinkle gelatin over the cold water and allow to dissolve. Meanwhile, combine grapefruit concentrate, sugar, salt, and 1 tablespoon of the lemon juice in a small saucepan. Stir in dissolved gelatin and simmer over medium heat for about 3 minutes.

Mix in grated lemon rind. Allow to cool and thicken slightly, then fold in whipped cream. Tie an oiled wax-paper collar around a 4-cup soufflé dish. Pour mixture in and refrigerate until set, several hours.

Crush the raspberries slightly and mix with the remaining tablespoon of lemon juice (and a little sweetener, if you desire). Do this just before serving. Spoon raspberries over each serving or pour them over the mousse and serve a bit of extra on the side.

Serves 6

Hazelnut Meringue Cookies with Mixed Fruit

Jean Thackery gave me the recipe for these cookies. They literally melt in your mouth. This is also a great way of using up extra egg whites.

    3 egg whites
    ½ teaspoon cream of tartar
    ⅛ teaspoon salt
    ¾ cup sugar
    2 cups coarsely ground hazelnuts

Preheat oven to 200 degrees. Lightly butter and flour (barely) a sheet of wax paper or baking parchment. Place on a cookie sheet.

Beat egg whites until stiff, adding cream of tartar and salt when foamy. Gradually stir in sugar. Fold in nuts.

Drop batter by tablespoonfuls onto the prepared paper. These do not rise or spread, so they may be placed fairly close together but not touching.

Bake for 1 hour and 15 minutes. Turn off oven and allow meringues to cool in the oven. Peel off paper and store in an airtight container.

Serve with mixed fresh fruit.

Makes approximately 36 cookies

Melon Balls with Cherries

When cherries are in season, I love serving them mixed with melon. I have a cherry pitter that makes fast work of them, but this is not really necessary. As a matter of fact, cherries look much more appealing with their stems on than they do with the pits removed.

Either way, select a nice, ripe melon such as a Santa Claus or a Honeydew, and cut it into cubes or make balls with a baller. I like the taste of cherries with these melons better than I do with cantaloupe. Give the whole thing a squeeze of lemon or lime juice and you are done. You might top it off with a bit of freshly grated lemon zest if you have the time and inclination.

Gingered Peaches with Pecan Tiles

You can substitute figs for the peaches here if they are in season. They are just as good, but probably more expensive unless you live in the South or West.

Pecan Tiles are a version of the famous French almond cookies that are, of course, fabulous with any poached fruit or ice cream.

    2½ cups water
     2 cups sugar
     3 tablespoons finely chopped peeled fresh ginger
     6 tree-ripened unblemished peaches

Mix water and sugar in a saucepan over medium heat. When simmering, add ginger. Simmer very slowly for 10 minutes.

Meanwhile, plunge peaches into boiling water for about 10 seconds and then slip off skins. Slide peaches into the boiling syrup and simmer slowly, carefully turning occasionally so peaches poach evenly. When tender —in about 10 minutes—allow to cool in the syrup. Transfer to a glass container with a slotted spoon and pour syrup over all. Refrigerate until ready to use. Serve with Pecan Tiles (recipe follows).

Serves 6

PECAN TILES

     2 egg whites
       Pinch of salt
    ½ teaspoon vanilla extract
    ½ cup superfine sugar
    ¼ cup plus 2 tablespoons all-purpose flour
    ¾ cup finely chopped pecans
     3 tablespoons unsalted butter, melted

Preheat oven to 375 degrees. Grease 2 cookie sheets.

Whip egg whites in a large bowl with the salt until foamy but not forming peaks. Fold in the vanilla and sugar.

Combine the flour with the pecans, mixing well. Sprinkle this over egg whites and incorporate. Stir in the butter. The batter should be liquid enough to spread out into a thin 3-inch circle when dropped onto the cookie sheet. If it is not, spread rounds with a small spatula.

Bake until golden brown around the edges, approximately 6 minutes. Drape each cookie over a rolling pin or the side of a wine bottle while it is still hot and pliable. Allow to remain there long enough to hold its "tile" shape. (If cookies get too hard before you can mold them all, place them back in the oven for another few seconds.)

Makes 18 to 24 cookies

SOME
GOOD
SALADS

Here are some things I don't like about salads: greens that have not been properly washed—I can't stand grit in a salad and won't eat it—and salad greens that have not been properly dried. With spinners for drying available every place these days, there is no excuse for it. If someone doesn't have a salad dryer, well, he or she must certainly have paper towels. Water clinging to greens dilutes the dressing, making it a mess.

While we are on the subject of messy salads, what about those presented swimming in dressing? Salads should be well dressed (no pun) so that the leaves are evenly coated, but not drenched. Add vinaigrette a few tablespoonfuls at a time, tossing between additions to enable you to check how you are doing, so you won't overdo. Add salt and a grinding of pepper then, too. Many people are surprised at how little vinaigrette is required to properly dress a salad.

A mess of another sort is those salads presented to you in restaurants all artfully (read: self-consciously) arranged in a bowl just large enough to hold the thing or spilling out over the edges. In this case the dressing is usually on the side. That's fine, but how are you going to toss it? The bowl isn't large enough, and it is presented in such a way as to imply that it is to be eaten from the bowl. And who wants to toss a salad themselves in a restaurant anyway? If you give up and just dump the dressing on top, you will have to wade through the soupy upper part before you get down to where there is a proper balance. Usually that strata is followed by one that has no dressing because it was all on top.

As I explain in the Sandwich section, it feels just great to get things like this off my chest!

Now on a more positive note, since I've already cautioned about the washing, drying, and dressing of salads, that leaves the combinations themselves. I like both extremes. A simple salad made of one main ingredient, such as watercress, arugula, or endive plus a small amount of another green (or not) is just fine with me. On the other hand, I equally enjoy salads made of every green in the garden, balancing a little of the bitter with the bland. You can also add all sorts of other elements, but when you start putting in too many things besides vegetables—such as ham, chicken, croûtons, nuts, and so on—you begin to create something that can be out of place if it is meant to be simply a pleasant transition to the dessert or a lead-in to the main course.

I must admit I've never been too keen on green salad as a first course, anyway.

And of course you can make salad of marinated vegetables, either lightly steamed or raw. There's lots to choose from.

There are, of course, times when nothing is quite as satisfying or appropriate as a plain green salad dressed with the simplest vinaigrette—as after a rich pasta or a heavy main-course soup. On such occasions I love the delicate sweet flavor of bibb lettuce tossed with the best olive oil and vinegar, a sprinkling of salt, and a grinding of pepper.

But there are also those times when salads that have a more complicated combination of flavors and textures are appropriate and are more substantial than palate cleansing. Here you may let your imagination take wing. This is the type of salad we are concerned with in this section.

As in the Sandwich section, my main intent is to get you thinking of alternatives to what often automatically comes to mind when you think "salad." For instance, how many of you toss pencil-thin fresh uncooked asparagus with your green salads, or add sliced uncooked mushrooms, or include walnuts or cubes of cheese? You see what I mean. These are not unknown salad ingredients, just overlooked ones. I'm not talking nasturtiums or rose petals here.

You might also want to consider experimenting with other oils as a change from the standard olive or vegetable oils. Try walnut, hazelnut, sesame, or a combination of one of these with a blander one such as corn oil. There are other oils like almond and grapeseed, but cut your teeth on the more readily available ones first.

And then there are the flavored (infused) oils. These are good, too, but save them for later as well.

As with oils, there is plenty of choice in vinegars. As an alternative to the old reliable red wine vinegar, many people have discovered the mellow, aromatic balsamic vinegar or are turning to rice vinegar or sherry vinegar and other types of wine vinegars.

Fruit vinegars are a very nice addition to salads and are easily made. For example, in the summer when I am up to my ears in raspberries, I simply fill a bottle with them, add white vinegar, and let it sit on a sunny windowsill for a couple of days before straining it. Delicious. Use any berry or soft fruit you like.

Onion Salads

Onions are the common ingredient in all the following salads. Obviously, if you don't like onions, or if you think your guests don't, these recipes are not for you.

Onion, Beet, and Endive Salad

It is so easy to bake fresh beets (see Lamb and Beet Soup, page 82) that you should avoid the canned variety whenever you can. Fresh ones have so much more flavor.

> Baked beets, trimmed, peeled, and quartered or cut into rings
> Red onions, sliced
> Endive leaves
> Balsamic vinaigrette
> Freshly ground pepper

Combine beets and onions with enough balsamic vinaigrette to flavor them nicely. Heap onto a bed of endive leaves and top with a grinding of black pepper.

Onion and Grapefruit Salad

Citrus fruits combine very well with onions. Just be sure to get as much of the white pith off as possible.

> Grapefruit sections, cut in half
> Sweet yellow (Vidalia) or red onions, cut into thin rings or chopped
> Sweet vinaigrette (see Note)
> Black olives, cured in oil
> Freshly ground black pepper

To remove the pith from peeled citrus, drop it whole for a few seconds into a pot of boiling water. This makes scraping off the excess pith easier. If you are ambitious you may even want to peel the individual sections. This is not as difficult as it sounds.

Toss the onions and grapefruit with the vinaigrette, garnish with black olives, and top with black pepper.

Note: For a sweet vinaigrette, add a little sugar or a sweet vinegar such as sherry. You may also add puréed fresh fruit directly to the vinaigrette—a puréed half-pear or berries stirred into basic vinaigrette. Also remember a few firm pieces of fruit tossed with garden greens, dressed with sesame dressing and topped with toasted sesame seeds, makes a pretty nifty salad, too.

Onion and Tomato Salad

This is another salad almost everyone has had.

> Vine-ripened tomatoes, peeled and thickly sliced
> Sweet yellow onions (Vidalia) or red onions, cut into medium rings, wilted (page 145) or raw
> Feta cheese, crumbled
> Fresh parsley, minced
> Mustard vinaigrette
> Freshly ground black pepper

Arrange tomato slices on individual plates. Top each with onions. Toss crumbled cheese and parsley together and sprinkle over all. Spoon a little mustard vinaigrette over the top and serve some on the side. Top with freshly ground black pepper.

Onion, Baby String Bean, and Toasted Pine Nut Salad

You may substitute asparagus here for the string beans.

> Small string beans, stemmed and tipped
> Sweet yellow onions (Vidalia), red onions, or green onions, coarsely chopped
> Red wine vinaigrette
> Toasted pine nuts
> Freshly ground black pepper

Steam beans until crisp-tender and allow to cool. Toss with the onions and a bit of red wine vinaigrette. Arrange on a plate and sprinkle pine nuts over all. Top with a grinding of black pepper.

Onion and Avocado Salad

This combination is a marriage made in heaven.

> Avocados, peeled, pitted, and cut into sixths or eighths
> Lemon juice
> Red wine vinaigrette
> Lettuce leaves
> Red onion, coarsely chopped
> Freshly ground black pepper

Rub avocado slices with the lemon juice (do not peel too far in advance). Toss with a little red wine vinaigrette and spoon onto lettuce leaves. Top with chopped onion and a few grindings of pepper.

Vegetable Salads

Many vegetables besides greens make perfect salads, either individually served raw or in combination.

Then there are the dried beans that can be cooked in the standard way and combined with fresh vegetables. They offer many possibilities as well.

Here are a few suggestions.

Cooked Vegetable Salad

As with any other vegetable salad, you can use almost any variety you like here. What follows is just a suggestion.

Vegetables may be lightly steamed or blanched. Dry well before using.

> Carrots, julienned
> Broccoli, cut into spears
> Asparagus
> String beans, tipped and stemmed
> Red bell peppers, roasted, peeled, and seeded
> Small new potatoes, boiled in their skins and cut in half
> Red wine vinaigrette
> Homemade Mayonnaise (page 6)

Either toss all the ingredients together with a little vinaigrette (mayonnaise on the side), or arrange on individual plates and serve with vinaigrette and mayonnaise on the side. I like both on my salad. I also feel a starchy vegetable, such as potato, provides a nice balance to this combination, as it does in the Summer Mélange.

Winter Vegetable Mélange

This is when I use dried beans. I often combine several kinds along with fresh vegetables, like so.

> White (navy) beans, cooked and drained
> Red kidney beans, cooked and drained
> Frozen corn kernels, steamed and cooled
> Onion, minced
> Green bell pepper, coarsely chopped
> Red wine vinaigrette
> Arugula
> Freshly ground black pepper

Toss all the vegetables, except the arugula, with a bit of red wine vinaigrette. Arrange arugula leaves on a plate and top with vegetables and a grind of black pepper.

Marinated Summer Mélange

During the middle of the warm months, when all sorts of young fresh vegetables are available, this is one of my favorite salads. You may use virtually any vegetable you like as long as it has a decent texture.

> Young string beans, stemmed, tipped, and broken in half
> Carrots, scraped and cut into ½-inch rings
> Zucchini, cut into ½-inch rings
> Red bell peppers, cut into thick strips
> Cauliflower, broken into small florets
> Celery, cut into thin pieces
> Red wine vinaigrette
> Lettuce leaves
> Small new potatoes, boiled in their jackets
> Green onions, coarsely chopped, with some green tops
> Tomato wedges

Toss together string beans, carrots, zucchini, peppers, cauliflower, and celery. Cover with vinaigrette and marinate overnight, covered; a glass jar with a seal top is a good container.

To serve, place lettuce on individual salad plates, with a few quartered small potatoes on top. Spoon the drained mixed vegetables over and top with chopped green onions. Garnish with tomato wedges.

Cheese with Salad

Finally, as everyone undoubtedly knows, a salad course may be made more substantial by serving cheese with it. To my way of thinking, the most successful combinations of salad and cheese are those in which the salad is a very simple green one dressed in the most basic way, giving the two elements a chance to complement each other.

Then there is another variation—that is, tossing a hard cheese like Parmesan, which has been shaved, with a single strong-flavored green such as arugula. This can be a delicious twosome. Another salad I like is shredded Swiss cheese and arugula combined with a strong, grainy mustard dressing.

Incidentally, using cheese in this way is different from making it an incidental ingredient in a larger, more complicated combination.

And everyone knows how good cheese is as part of a creamy dressing.

Black Bean and Macaroni Soup Lunch.

COLD-WEATHER MEALS

Cold-Weather Meals

I've found soup-making to be a particularly satisfying form of cold-weather cooking. For one thing, because the preparation of stocks and many dried-bean soups requires long simmering, soups are perfect to make when you must stay home working on some other project. For another, think how mouth-wateringly cozy the sautéeing onions and barely bubbling soups make the kitchen smell.

And of course, if you like soup and intend to have it often, you can get way ahead of the game by making stocks in large batches and freezing them in measured quantities to suit particular recipes.

However, if you don't want to bother with making stock (and don't feel guilty if you don't—I often don't either), you can use canned or instant powdered stock. Try a number of different brands to find one you like. I've found the flavor of some may be vastly improved by simmering them from 15 to 30 minutes with a little browned onion, carrot, and celery—which you then strain out before using.

The flavor of stocks can also be intensified by reducing them slightly, hence the name "rich" stock. Be aware that reducing canned stocks may make them more salty, depending on what brand is used.

That said, it may be worth making a stock once if you have never done so, first of all to find out if it is as difficult or time-consuming as you might think, and second, to have the flavor of something to compare the commercial ones against.

But whatever you do, always remember that the stock or liquid you use contributes mightily to the finished flavor (or lack of same) of most soups, consequently in many cases a soup cannot be much better than the flavor of the stock used to make it. This is especially true of soups requiring a limited number of ingredients.

Here are methods for making three basic stocks: chicken, beef, and vegetable. Frankly, I depend very heavily on chicken stock, which I use in many ways—not only for soup—so that is the one I concentrate on.

I'm including a recipe for vegetable stock, which I don't call for in any of my recipes but that actually can be substituted for chicken stock in many cases. If such a substitution doesn't work the way you imagine it will, just add a package or two of instant chicken stock to the whole thing. They'll never hear it from me if you do.

Chicken Stock

3 pounds chicken wings, backs, or other bones (see Note)
1 medium veal knuckle, cracked
4 quarts water
3 large onions, peeled and cut in half
2 large carrots, scrubbed and cut into large rings
2 medium leeks, carefully washed and cut into large rings
 Several large shallots, peeled but left whole
1 large bay leaf
8 parsley sprigs
8 large ribs celery with tops, broken into large pieces
1 teaspoon dried thyme
1 tablespoon salt
2 teaspoons freshly ground black pepper
1 whole clove

Select a stockpot large enough to comfortably hold all the above ingredients. Place the chicken, veal knuckle, and water in pot and bring to a boil. Skim foam, and add all the other ingredients. Bring back to a boil and reduce to the lowest possible heat; you want this to be barely simmering. Continue cooking for about 2½ hours, skimming occasionally as necessary.

Strain the cooked stock through a damp cheesecloth-lined colander. Discard all solids. Cool and refrigerate the stock. When fat has congealed on top, remove and discard it. The stock may be used as is or frozen.

Makes 3½ to 4 quarts

Note: Whenever I cook chicken, or fry chicken wings, I always cut off the tip joint and freeze it. There is a lot of gelatin in this (also in veal knuckle). And when I buy a whole chicken and am not cooking it whole, I usually freeze the back uncooked as well—unless I know a guest likes chicken backs. (My aunt Freddie does.) You will wind up with 3 pounds of uncooked chicken bones before you know it.

Beef Stock

5 pounds mixed beef and veal bones
2 large carrots, scrubbed
2 large ribs celery, cleaned
2 large onions, cut in half
   Water
2 tablespoons tomato paste
6 parsley sprigs
1 teaspoon leaf thyme
18 peppercorns
2 medium garlic cloves, crushed

Preheat oven to very hot, about 500 degrees. Place bones in a single layer in a roasting pan, break carrots and celery into large pieces and sprinkle among the bones, ditto with the onions. Roast for 30 to 45 minutes until meat, bones, and vegetables begin to brown, even burn a little. Dump these into a deep stock pot. Pour about a half inch of water into the roasting pan and dissolve any bits which have stuck to the bottom of the pan. Pour over bones. Add more water to several inches above bones. Bring to a boil and stir in tomato paste. Add parsley, thyme, peppercorns, and garlic. Cook, barely simmering, for several hours, adding more hot water as necessary. Strain and boil slowly until reduced and flavor is intensified. Allow to cool and skim any fat from the top. Refrigerate, tightly covered, or freeze.

Makes about 2 quarts

Vegetable Stock

1 tablespoon safflower oil
1 small onion, coarsely chopped
1 large leek, carefully washed and cut into large
   rings, some green
1 medium carrot, washed but not scraped, cut into
   large rings
¼ large bulb of fennel, you may use the tough outer
   layers, coarsely chopped
1 large rib celery, coarsely chopped, with some
   leaves
1 small tomato, coarsely chopped
⅛ very small head cabbage, coarsely chopped
10 cups water
1 bay leaf

Place oil in a deep pot and add the onion, leek, carrot, and fennel. Toss and cover tightly, cook over very low heat for about 5 minutes, shaking pan occasionally so as not to let vegetables scorch. Add celery, tomato, and cabbage. Toss again and cover tightly. Continue to cook over very low heat for an additional 10 minutes, shaking pan occasionally. Add water and bay leaf. Bring to a simmer and cook, barely simmering, for 30 minutes, skimming as necessary. Put ingredients through a strainer which has been lined with a double thickness of damp cheese cloth. Allow to cool and refrigerate, sealed, or freeze.

Makes about 1 quart

Note: You may make a heartier-flavored stock here by roasting the onion, leek, carrot, fennel, and celery, as in the beef stock recipe. When they have browned, add them with the dissolved pan juices to the other vegetables which you have sweated as in the second part of the Vegetable Stock recipe, then follow the balance of the recipe as above.

Above: Smoked Fish with Roasted Peppers and Zucchini.
Right: Turkey and Vegetable Soup with Mozzarella Biscuits.
Far right: Pecan Snickerdoodles with Mandarin Oranges.

Turkey and Vegetable Soup Lunch

The puréed raw green beans in this soup give it a nice fresh flavor. You could also make the whole thing with an uncooked chicken carcass or even by simmering a couple of chicken breasts in canned chicken stock. Anyway, it is a simple and satisfying soup to make once you gather the ingredients.

Equally easy mozzarella biscuits accompany the soup and, as a first course, you have a little composed dish of mixed temptations.

Finally, dessert consists of a favorite kids' cookie, snickerdoodles, enhanced by pecans served with mandarin orange sections splashed with grown-up liqueur.

Menu

Smoked Fish with Roasted Peppers and Zucchini
TURKEY AND VEGETABLE SOUP
Mozzarella Biscuits
Pecan Snickerdoodles with Mandarin Oranges
Wine
Coffee

Turkey and Vegetable Soup Lunch

Smoked Fish with Roasted Peppers and Zucchini

I am very fond of this sort of "composed" first course. You really could use any vegetable you like for this, from grilled asparagus to small new potatoes boiled in their skins. Pickles and olives may also be added. Check your refrigerator to see what you might find.

> ¾ to 1 pound smoked trout or other white fish, including head and tail
> 3 tablespoons prepared horseradish
> 1 tablespoon light cream
>   Lemon juice and grated lemon rind
> 3 small zucchini, split in half lengthwise
>   Olive oil
>   Freshly ground black pepper
>   Grated fresh Parmesan cheese
> 1 large red bell pepper, roasted, peeled, seeded, and cut into 6 wide strips

Garnish
> Endive leaves
> Lemon wedges, seeded

Slice fish across the backbone into sections several inches wide, discarding head and tail. Remove skin and place fish slices on individual plates. Mix horseradish and cream (or substitute a combination of mayonnaise and cream). Add lemon juice to taste. Top each section of fish with a dab of horseradish sauce and sprinkle with grated rind.

   Meanwhile, score cut zucchini and smear with olive oil. Sprinkle with pepper. Place under the broiler, and when they start turning golden, sprinkle with Parmesan. Place under broiler again until golden. Set aside. These should be served at room temperature.

   To serve, put half a zucchini on each plate with the fish and top with a strip of roasted pepper. Garnish with endive and lemon wedges, if desired.

Serves 6

Turkey and Vegetable Soup

A while back I started occasionally having my butcher slice fresh turkey breast for me to sauté instead of thin veal. This soup evolved from having the raw turkey breast carcass left over.

   Try having your butcher do the same.

   Incidentally, to cook the sliced breast, first lightly dust with flour, shaking off excess, then dip in beaten egg, allowing excess to drain off. Finally coat with fresh soft bread crumbs. Sauté in a combination of olive oil and butter. Top with your favorite tomato sauce or coulis.

> 2 tablespoons safflower oil
> 1 raw turkey breast carcass with meat on bones, chopped roughly into 4 or 5 pieces
> 7 cups Chicken Stock (page 74) or substitute turkey
> 4 cups water
> ½ very large red onion, peeled and thinly sliced
> 2 cups fresh green beens, puréed to the consistency of relish
> 2 large (1½ pounds) potatoes, peeled and cubed
> 4 large sprigs (without stems) parsley, chopped
> ½ teaspoon black pepper
> 1 (10-ounce) package frozen green peas

In the safflower oil, carefully and thoroughly brown (but do not burn) the turkey carcass parts and any bits of leftover raw meat. This may take about 5 minutes or more. Add stock and water. Bring to a simmer and continue to cook for about 40 minutes, skimming occasionally. Remove the bones and meat and let them cool. Remove meat from bones and chop coarsely. Discard bones.

   Add onion and green bean purée to the liquid and simmer over very low heat. Add potatoes and set timer for 5 minutes. Add parsley and pepper. (The pepper is very important here, so don't be shy about the amount.) Add reserved turkey meat and simmer just long enough to finish cooking the potatoes. Add peas and continue cooking for just a minute or so to heat them through.

Serves 8

Mozzarella Biscuits

If you have any of these easy little biscuits left over, you can warm them by placing them directly on the oven rack (not in a pan), so that the bottoms get crispy. I like them almost as well this way as I do when they first come out of the oven.

    2 cups all-purpose flour
    1 teaspoon salt
    2 teaspoons baking powder
    ½ teaspoon baking soda
    6 tablespoons (¾ stick) chilled unsalted butter, cut
      into pieces
 1½ cups buttermilk, approximately
    1 cup coarsely shredded mozzarella cheese

Preheat oven to 450 degrees.

Sift together the flour, salt, baking powder, and baking soda. Cut in butter with a pastry blender or 2 knives. Add enough buttermilk to make a thick dough. Stir in cheese. The dough should be thick enough so that it will just drop from a spoon with a little nudge.

Drop onto a well-greased baking sheet by the tablespoonful and bake for approximately 15 to 18 minutes. Remove with a spatula as soon as they come from the oven.

Makes 18 or more biscuits

Pecan Snickerdoodles with Mandarin Oranges

Snickerdoodles are almost my favorite simple cookie. No wonder they have been so popular over the years. If you like, you can lightly press a small pecan half on top of each ball of dough just before baking (in addition to the pecans already in the dough) to make these a little more decorative.

Orange sections are always welcome. Get seedless oranges if you can.

    1 cup plus 6 tablespoons all-purpose flour
    1 teaspoon cream of tartar
    ½ teaspoon baking soda
      Pinch of salt
    ½ cup (1 stick) unsalted butter, softened
    ¾ cup sugar plus 2 tablespoons
    1 egg

    1 cup very coarsely chopped toasted pecans
 1½ teaspoons ground cinnamon
      Seedless mandarin orange sections
      Grand Marnier liqueur

Sift together the flour, cream of tartar, baking soda, and salt. Set aside.

In a large bowl, cream the butter and ¾ cup of sugar until light and fluffy. Beat in the egg. Beat in the flour mixture, in 4 parts, until thoroughly mixed. Stir in pecans. Wrap dough in wax paper and refrigerate for at least 1 hour.

When ready to bake, preheat the oven to 400 degrees. Mix the remaining 2 tablespoons of sugar and the cinnamon on a sheet of wax paper. Pinch off pieces of chilled dough and roll each into a walnut-size (or smaller) ball. Roll each in the sugar-cinnamon to coat. Place on an ungreased cookie sheet, 2 inches apart, and bake for 10 minutes. Remove to a rack to cool.

Serve with seedless mandarin orange sections (remove as much white pith as possible) sprinkled with a bit of Grand Marnier. You can also serve extra Grand Marnier on the side.

Makes 24 or more cookies

Here's How

For the soup, you can make the basic chicken stock with the carcass several days ahead if you like. Plan to have all the other ingredients sliced, diced, etc., and then finish the soup just before you stir up the biscuits.

All the ingredients for the biscuits can be mixed ahead of time except for the buttermilk, and placed in the refrigerator earlier in the day. Then it will take only minutes to complete them for baking.

Obviously, you can make the cookies the day before if you like. And you can also roast the pepper, mix the horseradish sauce, and grate the lemon rind then for the first course.

Broil the zucchini so it will be finished by the time guests are due to arrive. Prepare the oranges about then as well.

The whole menu is pretty flexible, so be relaxed about it all.

Lamb and Beet Soup Lunch

When you read the ingredients that go into this soup you will recognize them as those often found in borscht —which isn't exactly bad. The twist here is the use of marinated lamb as the soup's base to create the tasty broth.

However, you have to love the flavor of beets, as I do, to go for this soup. Beets have such a strong and distinctive flavor that they dominate almost any dish they are a part of.

Served with the soup are coarse bran muffins, and for a first course, there is a spicy veal and chicken terrine.

Finally, the meal is completed with fig custard.

All in all, it's a hearty lunch to fortify you and guests against winter's chill.

Menu

Veal and Chicken Terrine
LAMB AND BEET SOUP
Bran Muffins
Fresh Fig Baked Custard
Wine
Coffee

Lamb and Beet Soup with Bran Muffins.
Opposite, top: Veal and Chicken Terrine.
Opposite, bottom: Fresh Fig Baked Custard.

Lamb and Beet Soup Lunch

Veal and Chicken Terrine

Serve this the way you would any traditional pâté, with a bit of mustard, a few cornichons or olives, and toasted thin-sliced bread.

12 ounces boneless chicken, cubed
2 teaspoons coarsely chopped shallots
1 tablespoon finely minced garlic
½ teaspoon paprika
½ teaspoon white pepper
1 teaspoon salt
¼ teaspoon grated nutmeg
½ teaspoon black peppercorns, crushed
1 pound very coarsely ground veal
3 thick slices bacon, cubed

Preheat oven to 350 degrees.

Place chicken, shallots, garlic, and spices in a food processor and process until well mixed. Combine this mixture with the peppercorns, ground veal, and bacon in another bowl. Mix well with your hands. Pat into a 4-cup ceramic baking crock. Smooth top and bake in a water bath until firm, about 45 minutes. Allow to cool completely before refrigerating, covered.

Serves 6 to 8

Lamb and Beet Soup

4 thick shoulder lamb chops, a generous 2 pounds

Marinade
5 tablespoons bourbon
¼ cup soy sauce
¼ cup light brown sugar, tightly packed
2 tablespoons olive oil
3 tablespoons Dijon mustard
1 teaspoon Worcestershire sauce
1 teaspoon black pepper
½ teaspoon salt
⅛ teaspoon cayenne (ground red) pepper
½ medium onion, coarsely sliced

1 pound trimmed fresh beets, with 1 inch of tops
4 cups water
2 cups Beef Stock (page 75)
1 large onion, coarsely chopped
4 medium carrots, peeled; 1 cut into large rounds and 3 coarsely grated
3 large sprigs parsley
½ teaspoon dried thyme
1 large bay leaf
½ pound green cabbage, cored and thinly shredded
1 (1-pound) can peeled tomatoes, thoroughly drained
2 tablespoons red wine vinegar
½ teaspoon salt
½ teaspoon black pepper
2 large baking potatoes (about 1¼ pounds), peeled and cubed
3 tablespoons chopped fresh dill (no stems)
  Sour cream
  Chopped fresh chives

Place chops in a shallow glass or ceramic dish in a single layer. Mix marinade ingredients thoroughly and pour over all, allowing the onion to remain on top. This liquid should cover the chops. Cover with foil wrap and refrigerate overnight. Turn once.

Lift the chops out of the marinade, leaving onion on top, and place in a shallow baking pan in a cold oven. Turn the oven on to 350 degrees and bake for 1½ hours, turning chops once.

Place beets in a foil-lined pan and cover with foil. Put in the oven with the chops. When chops are done, remove. Test beets for doneness. If not tender, turn oven up to 400 degrees and continue to cook until they can be pierced easily with the point of a knife. When beets are tender, peel and chop into small dice. Set aside.

Meanwhile, place chops in a large pot along with any pan juice, degreased. Add water, stock, onion, carrot rounds, parsley, thyme, and bay leaf. Simmer, uncovered, over very low heat for 1 hour.

Remove lamb and cut into strips or cubes, discarding any fat, gristle, and bone. Set aside.

Strain pot liquid. Discard vegetables and return liquid to the pot. Add beets, grated carrots, cabbage, tomatoes, vinegar, salt, and pepper. Simmer for 30 minutes, adding lamb after about 15 minutes.

While this is simmering, boil the potatoes in salted water until fork-tender, about 10 to 12 minutes. Drain and set aside.

To serve, ladle soup into bowls and place a few cooked potatoes in the middle. Sprinkle generously with chopped dill before adding a dollop of sour cream topped with chives. Serve additional dill and sour cream on the side.

Serves 6

Bran Muffins

I am very fond of the texture of these coarse muffins with the beet soup. They are a pleasant alternative to the dark bread usually served with it.

2¾ cups bran flakes
¼ cup light brown sugar, tightly packed
½ cup whole wheat flour
½ cup all-purpose flour
2 teaspoons baking powder
1 teaspoon salt
¾ cup sour cream
3 eggs
3 tablespoons unsalted butter, melted

Preheat oven to 400 degrees. Generously grease 12 medium muffin cups.

Place the bran flakes in a food processor and process until the flakes are coarsely ground. This should yield approximately 1 cup powder, which is what you need. In a large bowl, mix bran with the brown sugar and set aside. Sift the flours, baking powder, and salt together. Combine thoroughly with the bran mixture.

Beat the sour cream and eggs together, then pour into the dry ingredients. Stir and add butter, then stir just to mix; don't overmix. Fill cups about ¾ full, and bake for about 20 minutes.

Makes 12 muffins

Fresh Fig Baked Custard

I know figs are expensive during the colder months, but it really doesn't take too many to make a cup, and that's all you need here.

1 cup sugar
6 tablespoons all-purpose flour
2½ teaspoons baking powder
Pinch of salt
2 eggs, lightly beaten
1 teaspoon vanilla extract
1 teaspoon bourbon
1 cup chopped pecans
1 cup stemmed and mashed fresh figs
1 teaspoon grated fresh lemon rind
Heavy cream (optional)

Preheat oven to 350 degrees. Generously butter an 8-inch square baking pan. Set aside.

Mix sugar, flour, baking powder, and salt in a large bowl. Combine beaten egg, vanilla, and bourbon. Pour into dry ingredients, stirring. Add pecans, figs, and lemon rind. Continue to mix (with a hand mixer) until very well blended, several minutes.

Pour and scrape mixture into prepared pan and bake for 30 to 35 minutes, or until a knife inserted in middle comes out clean.

Serve as is, or with a topping of heavy cream, either whipped or not.

Serves 6

Here's How

You can prepare the soup well in advance, up to the point of adding the carrots and cabbage. Then when you reheat it prior to serving, put the vegetables in.

The terrine could also be prepared ahead; and even the fig custard might be done earlier in the day. But I don't think I would make the custard ahead unless there were no other time to fix it.

Bran muffins, like almost all muffins, are so easy to put together and are so much better if eaten when they first come from the oven that you should serve them hot when you can. To do this, have all the ingredients measured and ready, and then put them in the oven to bake while you're having the first course.

Turnip and Acorn Squash Soup Lunch

Above: Duck Sausage and New Potatoes.
Below: Grape Tart with Red Currant Glaze.
Right: Turnip and Acorn Squash Soup.

Turnip and Acorn Squash Soup Lunch

I'm always trying new combinations of vegetables to make soup. And with a food processor, the task is made even easier. I also like such soups to be rather thick, as you will notice this one is; however, if this texture doesn't suit you, by all means thin the soup with a little milk or more stock. Sometimes doing this requires that you correct the seasoning. I'm not too keen on heavily creamed soups, so I seldom use heavy cream—but there is always the delectable exception; see Sweet Potato Vichyssoise on page 55.

The soup this time is served with big fried croûtons.

For a first course there are sausages and new potatoes—a combination I'm particularly fond of. I've given my recipe for duck sausage, but you may substitute a commercial one if you are pressed for time or simply not in the mood for sausage making.

Finally, the dessert is a delightful grape tart.

Menu

> *Duck Sausage and New Potatoes*
> *TURNIP AND ACORN SQUASH SOUP*
> *Fried Croûtons*
> *Grape Tart with Red Currant Glaze*
> *Wine*
> *Coffee*

Duck Sausage and New Potatoes

Sausage making can be fun and is easy to personalize when you alter the kind, quantities, and proportions of herbs used. Always make this far enough in advance to give it a day or so in the refrigerator for the flavors to develop.

    1 pound duck meat (no skin or fat), cut into large
       cubes
    4 ounces duck fat (see Note)
   10 juniper berries, crushed
    ½ teaspoon ground dried thyme
    ⅛ teaspoon ground sage
    ½ teaspoon coarsely ground black pepper
    1 teaspoon salt
   18 small new potatoes
       Butter

Place duck meat and fat in a food processor and chop coarsely. Do not overprocess. Mix in other ingredients (except potatoes and butter) with your hands, being sure they are well combined. To check seasoning, fry a small amount of the sausage, starting it in a cold skillet. Refrigerate overnight, covered, to allow flavors to meld.

Form into patties and fry as above.

Serve with freshly boiled, unpeeled new potatoes, buttered.

Serves 6

Note: If you come up short on duck fat, add chicken fat to make up the difference.

Turnip and Acorn Squash Soup

As you might imagine, this has a pronounced turnip flavor. If turnips are not one of your favorite vegetables, maybe this soup is not for you. But you can cut down on the turnip flavor by reducing their number or by adding a cubed small potato to the combination.

Anyway, as I pointed out earlier, this is the sort of soup that invites innovation.

    ¼ cup (½ stick) unsalted butter (or half butter, half
       margarine)
    8 ounces coarsely chopped, well-washed leeks,
       white part only (about 2 cups)
    4 ounces coarsely chopped onion
   2½ ounces coarsely grated carrot (about ¾ cup)
    1 small garlic clove, cut into several pieces
    1 teaspoon sugar
    1 large acorn squash (1½ pounds), split and seeded,
       cut surface rubbed with a little butter
   10 ounces white turnip, peeled
    5 cups rich Chicken Stock (page 74)
       Generous ¼ teaspoon white pepper
    1 teaspoon salt
       Scant ¼ teaspoon ground coriander
       Crème fraîche or sour cream

Preheat oven to 375 degrees.

Melt butter in a stockpot and toss with leeks, onion, carrot, and garlic. Sprinkle sugar over all and cover tightly. Sweat over lowest possible heat for 20 minutes. Do not allow to burn.

Place squash in a foil-lined pan and bake until fork-tender, about 30 minutes.

When vegetables are cooked, add turnips and 2 cups of the stock, plus white pepper, salt, and coriander. Simmer until turnips are tender, about 20 minutes. Transfer vegetables and liquid to a food processor. Scoop out pulp of acorn squash and add to vegetables. Purée all and return to pot. Stir in balance of the stock and heat. Correct seasoning if necessary. Serve with a dollop of crème fraîche or sour cream.

Serves 6 to 8

Fried Croûtons

These croûtons are not the small cubes of toast that you find in salads or floating on top of soup. Instead, they are slices of French or Italian bread that have been fried until golden and crisp.

To make them, simply cut a loaf of French or Italian bread on a diagonal with a serrated knife into ¾-inch slices. Butter both sides lightly with softened unsalted butter. Set aside.

Put ½ cup of good-quality olive oil in a large skillet and mash about 6 cloves of garlic into it as the oil heats. When the garlic begins to brown, discard. Pour oil out and reserve, leaving a thin coating on the bottom of the pan. Turn heat to medium and fry the bread slices, turning as necessary. Add more oil and continue frying the bread until all have been done. Serve warm or at room temperature.

Grape Tart with Red Currant Glaze

The best kind of grapes to use for this are the medium-size seedless red ones or the Champagne grapes one sees in the markets these days.

  1 cup all-purpose flour
  ⅓ cup confectioners' sugar
  ½ cup (1 stick) unsalted butter, softened
  2 tablespoons granulated sugar
  1 egg
  ¾ cup sour cream
  1 large bunch seedless grapes
    Juice of ½ small lemon
  ½ cup red currant jelly, heated
    Cream, flavored with sugar, rum, bourbon, or vanilla

Preheat oven to 350 degrees.

Place flour, confectioners' sugar, and butter in a mixing bowl and, using your fingers, work it to form a stiff dough. Press and pat it into the bottom of a 4½ × 14-inch tart pan. It is not necessary to line the sides.

Mix granulated sugar, egg, and sour cream and spread over the dough. Arrange grapes in an even layer over the sour cream mixture. Sprinkle with lemon juice.

Bake until the dough is done and turning golden around the edges, about 50 minutes.

Let tart cool for about 10 minutes, then loosen around the edges and slide off onto a tart plate. Spread heated jelly over all and smooth evenly (with your fingers, if necessary). Serve with flavored cream.

Serves 6 to 8

Here's How

The soup may be made well in advance, if you like. This goes for the basic sausage preparation, too.

Even the bread can be fried in the afternoon. However, if you do this, don't reheat it for too long in the oven, or you will dry it out. On the other hand, if you like dry toast . . .

When you are ready to serve, put the soup in a double boiler over boiling water, the potatoes in a pot of water, and the sausage patties in a cold skillet. None of these dishes is temperamental, so they should all be ready about the same time.

As for the dessert, it is best if it is not made too far in advance, since the crust will deteriorate somewhat. Time it to come out of the oven about when the guests are due to arrive if you can swing it, or as close to then as possible.

Black Bean and Macaroni Soup Lunch

Below: Duck and Pork Rillettes. Bottom: Walnut Cake with Rum Cream. Opposite: Black Bean and Macaroni Soup.

Since this is a pretty stick-to-your-ribs combination of dishes, it should be served for a late Sunday lunch or an early supper, not as your everyday kind of midday repast.

Actually, the soup is probably the simplest thing about this whole meal. But since the other courses can be made—at least in part—well in advance, it is perfect for one of those weekends when the blustery weather invites you to stay inside rather than to venture out.

You begin the meal with rillettes, which is a pâté-like dish. You could serve this on water wafers or toast with before-lunch drinks in the living room, if you like.

The dessert is a real treat. I know I am always saying this to people about the various dishes I cook, but you'll love this one. Trust me.

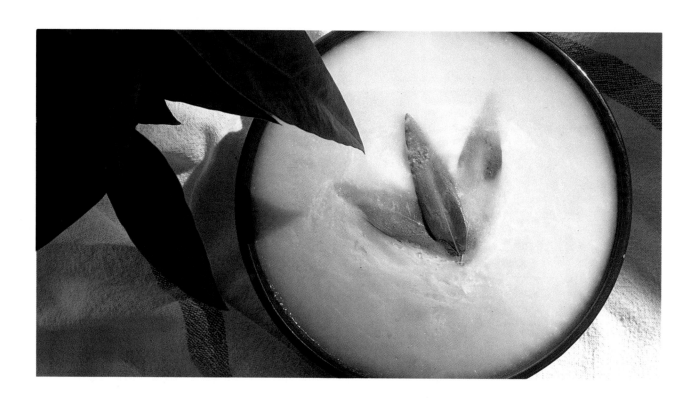

Menu

Duck and Pork Rillettes
BLACK BEAN AND MACARONI SOUP
Thin Cornbread
Walnut Cake with Rum Cream
Wine
Coffee

Black Bean and Macaroni Soup Lunch

Duck and Pork Rillettes

Rillettes are usually made with pork only, but the duck is a pleasant change.

    2 pounds boneless salt pork (no rind), cut into ½-inch cubes
    1 pound lean pork, cut into large cubes
    1 pound boned duck meat and neck
    1 teaspoon black pepper
    1 teaspoon dried rosemary
    ½ teaspoon dried thyme
    1 cup water
    ¼ cup cognac
      Bouquet garni of 3 large peeled shallots,
      1 crushed large garlic clove, 1 large bay leaf,
      1 tablespoon juniper berries

Preheat oven to 350 degrees.

Cover salt pork cubes with cold water and blanch for 5 minutes. Drain.

Place all ingredients, including salt pork, in a cast-iron pot and bring to a boil on top of the stove. Skim foam and cover tightly. Bake in the oven, covered, for 3 to 3½ hours. Uncover and continue baking until all the liquid has evaporated, leaving only the meat and fat; this should take an additional 25 to 30 minutes.

Drain off fat, pressing it out of the meat lightly. When cool enough to handle, pull meat apart, discarding any bone and skin. Discard bay leaf and garni. Process the meat in small batches very briefly in the food processor. You want this to be chunky. Pack into a crock and chill. Heat fat and pour over chilled meat. Place a bay leaf in the fat for decoration, if you like.

Keeps in the refrigerator for up to 1 month if tightly sealed and covered with fat.

Serve with Melba Toast (page 7).

Makes about 2 pounds

Black Bean and Macaroni Soup

I am especially fond of the combination of beans and macaroni. And with sweet red peppers—oh, boy!

    1 cup dried black beans
    8 cups Chicken Stock (page 74), approximately
    2 small bay leaves
    ¼ cup olive oil
    1 large onion, coarsely chopped
    1 small garlic clove, finely chopped
    1 cup drained and chopped canned tomatoes (not in paste)
    2 tablespoons red wine
    1 teaspoon sugar
    ¼ teaspoon black pepper
    1½ cups elbow macaroni
    2 very large red bell peppers, roasted, peeled, and cut into medium dice

Garnish
    Finely chopped flat-leaf parsley and green onion

Wash and pick over beans. Cover with an inch of water and bring to a rapid boil. Boil for 2 minutes and turn off heat. Allow to sit, covered, for 1 hour.

Drain beans and cover with 3 cups of the chicken stock. Bring to a boil and turn heat down to a simmer. Add bay leaves. Simmer until the beans start to get tender, about 1 hour and 30 minutes.

Meanwhile, heat the olive oil and sauté the onion until wilted and starting to brown, about 5 minutes. Stir in the garlic and continue to cook for another minute or so. Scrape the onion-garlic mixture into the beans and add the tomatoes. Continue cooking, adding more stock if necessary, until beans are done. This can take up to another hour. Add wine, sugar, pepper, and balance of the stock.

To serve, boil macaroni in very well salted water for 6 minutes. Drain and add to the bean mixture along with the diced red pepper. Simmer just long enough to completely cook the macaroni. Allow to sit for about 5 minutes before serving. This probably will not need salt, but correct seasoning if necessary.

If you have cooked the soup too rapidly you may have evaporated too much of the liquid. In that case, add a bit more stock. However, this should be a very thick soup.

Sprinkle with chopped flat-leaf parsley and green onion, if desired.

Serves 6

Thin Cornbread

Since the crust of cornbread is my favorite part, I always make it thin so I'll wind up with mostly crust. For those of you who don't care, you may certainly make this in one skillet instead of two.

> 3 tablespoons safflower oil
> 2 cups white cornmeal
> 4 teaspoons baking powder
> 1½ teaspoons salt
> 1 egg
> 1½ cups milk

Preheat oven to 450 degrees. Place two 10-inch cast-iron skillets in the oven as it is heating.

When oven is ready, remove heated skillets and divide the safflower oil between the two. Quickly swirl oil around and put skillets back in the oven.

Sift the cornmeal, baking powder, and salt together. Drop the egg into the milk and mix well. Pour into meal mixture. Mix quickly.

Pour half the batter into each skillet and bake until golden, about 20 minutes. Serve with sweet butter.

Serves 6

Note: This bread reheats very well. To do so, place it directly on the rack of a preheated 300 degree oven and leave it there just long enough for it to heat through and for the bottom to crisp up. If you put it on a cookie sheet for reheating, the bottom will not be crisp.

Walnut Cake with Rum Cream

This cake may be made with pecans or any combination of nuts you might like.

> 1½ cups all-purpose flour
> 1 teaspoon baking powder
> ½ teaspoon salt
> 1½ cups finely chopped or grated walnuts
> ½ cup (1 stick) unsalted butter, softened
> 1¾ cups plus 2 tablespoons sugar
> ¼ cup rum mixed with ½ cup water
> 4 egg whites
> 1 teaspoon powdered espresso (optional)

Rum Cream
> 1 pint heavy cream
> 2 teaspoons rum

Preheat oven to 375 degrees. Grease two square 8-inch cake pans and cut wax paper to fit the bottoms of each. Grease paper and then lightly flour the whole inside.

In a medium bowl, sift together the flour, baking powder, and salt. Add the walnuts and mix well. Set aside.

In a large bowl, cream the butter and 1½ cups of the sugar until light and fluffy, about 5 minutes. Add the flour-walnut mixture in 4 parts, alternating with the rum water and beginning and ending with the flour. Mix well after each addition.

In a large bowl, beat the egg whites until stiff. Fold one-third of the egg whites into the cake batter to lighten it and then fold in the remaining egg whites. Pour into prepared pans and bake until a cake tester comes out clean, approximately 25 minutes.

When cakes are done, allow to cool in the pans for about 10 minutes. Then run a knife around the edges and unmold onto a cooling rack. When cakes are completely cooled, remove wax paper from the bottoms.

Whip cream and stir in the balance of the sugar and the rum. Pile half the cream on one of the layers and top it with the other layer (held in place with toothpicks, if necessary). Pile the balance of the cream on top. Sprinkle with powdered espresso, if desired.

Serves 6 to 8

Here's How

You can make the rillettes well in advance of the time you serve it; as a matter of fact, it is better if it has time to mature in the refrigerator for a week or so.

The soup can be made the day before, but don't add the macaroni and peppers until you are ready to serve. The cornbread can be made the day before as well and reheated. (See the recipe for instructions.)

The cake, too, may be made a day or so in advance. Wrap the layers well after they have cooled. Do the whipped cream filling and assemble in the late afternoon of the day it is to be served, and keep refrigerated, with wax paper or plastic wrap draped over the top.

Above: Chicken and Dill Soup. Right:
Fettuccine with Greens and Pine Nuts.
Opposite: Honey-Banana Ice Cream.

Chicken and Dill Soup Lunch

There have been so many jokes made about the medicinal value of chicken soup that I think people sometimes forget just how satisfying it really is and how easy to make.

A very good soup may be made by slowly simmering a large chicken along with vegetables and herbs. But here I've taken another tack on the old stalwart. It's still easy, but I prefer cooking the chicken separately and adding it last.

To begin this little lunch is another of everyone's favorites, pasta. Here it is dressed with garlic oil and greens and topped by pine nuts.

For a surprise, popovers are served with the soup—but not just plain popovers, pecan popovers.

Dessert is built around honey.

Menu

Fettuccine with Greens and Pine Nuts
CHICKEN AND DILL SOUP
Pecan Popovers
Honey-Banana Ice Cream
Honey-Peanut Cookies
Wine
Coffee

Chicken and Dill Soup Lunch

Fettuccine with Greens and Pine Nuts

Almost all greens are delicious as far as I'm concerned, and broccoli rabe is one of the best. Its flavor is strong, and here is enhanced by garlic oil. The only problem is getting the chopped, cooked rabe dispersed evenly with the pasta. Use 2 forks and a little patience for this.

I think this is better without the traditional Parmesan cheese.

    1½ pounds broccoli rabe
     1 tablespoon instant chicken stock
     ⅛ teaspoon dried red pepper flakes
       Salt to taste
     ½ pound fettuccine
     ¼ cup good-quality olive oil
     2 large garlic cloves, finely minced (not in a garlic press)
       Approximately 3 ounces or more pine nuts, darkly toasted

Cut large stems from broccoli rabe and discard. Place in a very large container of water and let soak. Carefully lift rabe from the water, giving it a few shakes, and place in a large, deep pot with just the water clinging to the leaves. Sprinkle instant stock over all. Cover and cook until tender, about 8 minutes, depending on the age of the rabe. Stir and turn over several times during the cooking and shake the pan back and forth. When cooked, quickly boil off the liquid (uncovered). If this takes too long, pour out liquid. Add pepper flakes and toss. Salt to taste. Using 2 knives, chop the broccoli rabe into coarse bits.

To serve, cook fettuccine until just al dente. Meanwhile, warm the olive oil and add the garlic. Warm for 10 minutes, covered, to flavor the oil. Do not cook. Turn up heat and sauté, uncovered, for a few minutes until garlic is just starting to turn color. Stir and pour over the broccoli rabe. Toss with the fettuccine. Top each serving with pine nuts.

Serves 6

Chicken and Dill Soup

The amount of dill called for in this recipe gives this soup a fairly mild dill flavor. Frankly, when I make it for myself I use almost double the amount. If you really like the flavor of dill, as I obviously do, you might want to increase the amount, too.

    2½ pounds chicken breast (2 large breasts),
       split in half
       Salt
       Black pepper
     2 very large onions (1¼ pounds), chopped very coarsely
     6 cups Chicken Stock (page 74)
     6 ounces carrots, cut into rounds (about 1½ cups)
     ¾ pound baking potato, peeled and diced
     1 teaspoon salt
     ¼ teaspoon black pepper
     ¼ teaspoon dried thyme
       Scant ¼ teaspoon ground mace
     3 generous tablespoons chopped fresh dill (no stems)

Preheat oven to 375 degrees.

Salt and pepper the chicken breasts generously. Spread half the chopped onions on the bottom of a baking dish large enough to hold the chicken breasts in a single layer. Put the balance of the onions on top of the chicken. Bake, uncovered, for 15 minutes. Heat 1 cup of the chicken stock and pour into pan. Bake another 20 minutes. Turn off heat and allow to continue cooking by retained heat for another hour. Chicken may rest in the oven for several hours.

Remove bones and skin from chicken and discard. Set chicken aside.

Strain the baked onions from the pan juices. Place drained onions in a large pot with the balance of the stock. Heat. Meanwhile, degrease pan juices and add to pot along with all other ingredients. Simmer for 8 minutes, skimming if necessary. When carrots and potato are almost fork-tender, cut chicken into large cubes and add. Turn off heat and allow to sit for about 15 minutes before serving.

Serves 6 to 8

Pecan Popovers

The important thing here is to make sure the pecans are finely chopped, otherwise they will not mix throughout.

   6 tablespoons all-purpose flour
   1 cup plus 2 tablespoons finely chopped pecans
   ¼ teaspoon salt
   1½ cups milk
   3 eggs, lightly beaten
   1 tablespoon plus 1½ teaspoons butter, melted and
      cooled

Preheat oven to 450 degrees. Generously butter twelve ½-cup custard cups.

   Mix flour and pecans in a large bowl. Add salt. Mix in milk, eggs, and cooled butter. Stir, but do not overmix. Pour into prepared custard cups, filling each about three-fourths full. Place on a cookie sheet and bake for 15 minutes.

   Turn heat to 350 degrees and bake another 20 minutes. Do not open oven while cooking, but check temperature before you start to make sure it's correct.

   As soon as you remove the popovers from the oven, puncture sides with a knife to let any steam out. This will prevent them from collapsing. Serve immediately.

Makes 12 popovers

Honey-Banana Ice Cream

I am especially fond of honey flavor in ice cream.

   1 cup heavy cream
   1 cup milk
   ⅔ cup honey
   3 egg yolks, room temperature
      Pinch of salt
   1 cup mashed ripe bananas

Combine cream and milk in a saucepan. Slowly cook over moderate heat until heated, 2 minutes. Off heat, add honey and mix until completely dissolved. Set aside.

   Beat egg yolks with salt until frothy. Add ½ cup of the honey-cream mixture to heat yolks. Return pan to low heat and add yolks. Stirring all the while, cook until mixture coats the back of a spoon, several minutes.

   Pour into an ice-cream maker and freeze according to manufacturer's directions until it begins to thicken. Mix in mashed bananas and finish freezing.

Makes approximately 1½ pints

Honey-Peanut Cookies

If you are not crazy about peanuts, you may certainly use another kind of nut in this recipe.

   1¼ cups sugar
   ¾ cup (1½ sticks) unsalted butter, softened
   1 egg
   ¼ cup honey
   2 cups all-purpose flour
   2 teaspoons baking soda
   ½ teaspoon salt
   2 teaspoons ground allspice
   1 teaspoon ground cinnamon
   ½ teaspoon grated nutmeg
   ¼ teaspoon ground cloves
   1 teaspoon black pepper
   1½ cups dry-roasted peanuts, ½ cup finely chopped

Preheat oven to 350 degrees.

   Cream ¾ cup of the sugar and the butter until fluffy. Beat in egg and then add honey. Combine flour with the other dry ingredients and sift. Add the flour mixture to the batter and mix well. Fold in whole peanuts.

   Mix remaining sugar with chopped peanuts. Form dough into 1-inch balls and roll in sugar-peanut mixture. Place 2 inches apart on an ungreased cookie sheet.

   Bake until lightly browned, about 15 to 18 minutes.

Makes 24 to 30 cookies

Here's How

Dessert can be made any time you can get to it. The baking of the chicken and onions for the soup essence can be made in advance too, even several days before. If you do this, wait to add the potato, carrots, and dill until you are getting the pasta for the first course ready. These vegetables only cook 8 minutes before you turn the whole thing off.

   Have popover ingredients ready; when they go in the oven, put the chicken in the soup pot and have your first course. You'll have to get back into the kitchen to turn the oven down halfway through the popover baking.

   Of course, popovers should be eaten hot, so the final timing should be built around them.

   Make the pasta sauce ahead and reheat it. The timing of the soup and popovers gives you almost 25 minutes to finish the first course.

   If you don't want to be bothered with this simple timing, substitute crisp bread and make the popovers for some other meal (Sunday breakfast?).

Steak and Mushroom Soup Dinner

Left: Steak and Mushroom Soup with Buttermilk Drop Biscuits. _Above:_ Baked Potatoes with Caviar. _Below:_ Pear Pudding Cake.

Steak and Mushroom Soup Dinner

Now here is a menu for the meat and potatoes crowd—in a slightly glamourized version. It begins with a baked potato, but not just an ordinary baked potato, rather one dressed with a generous dollop of caviar. And the soup has cubes of marinated steak and plenty of fresh mushrooms in it, accompanied by old-fashioned drop buttermilk biscuits.

For dessert is an equally old-fashioned pear pudding cake.

Menu

Baked Potatoes with Caviar
STEAK AND MUSHROOM SOUP
Buttermilk Drop Biscuits
Pear Pudding Cake
Wine
Coffee

Baked Potatoes with Caviar

I assume that almost everyone knows how to bake a potato, but I am amazed at how often people do the one or two things that diminish their delicious natural flavor and texture. Personally, I love the crunch and taste of the skin after it has been baked, and it is here where most of the mistakes seem to be made.

First, the potato should be baked in a very hot oven, say 425 degrees. But before it goes in, it should be well washed and dried, then rubbed generously with vegetable oil and sprinkled with salt. Don't ever wrap the potato in foil. *This absolutely ruins the texture of the skin, which should be dry and crunchy.*

6 medium baking potatoes, washed and dried
Safflower oil
Salt
Unsalted butter
Freshly ground black pepper
Caviar
Chopped green onions or chives

Preheat the oven to 425 degrees. Generously rub the potatoes with vegetable oil and sprinkle with salt. Bake for approximately 40 minutes to 1 hour, depending on size.

Split each potato down the center and press open. Spread with a generous amount of butter, sprinkle with fresh pepper, and top with caviar. Sprinkle a few chopped green onions or chives over the top.

Serves 6

Steak and Mushroom Soup

I think marinating the steak improves its flavor; however, if you are rushed you might try it without this step.

1¼ pounds thick shell steak, trimmed and cut into 1-inch cubes
3 tablespoons olive oil
3 tablespoons unsalted butter
3 medium onions, half coarsely chopped, other half thinly sliced
2 small carrots, scraped and finely chopped
2 small ribs celery, finely chopped
1 pound fresh button mushrooms, thickly sliced
Flour for dusting
5 to 6 cups Beef Stock (page 75)
1½ teaspoons salt
Generous ¼ teaspoon freshly ground black pepper
1 large bay leaf
1¼ pounds escarole, washed and torn into bite-size pieces, with stems broken

Marinade
⅔ cup safflower oil
2 tablespoons lemon juice
1 tablespoon dark brown sugar
2 tablespoons dark soy sauce
1 teaspoon Dijon mustard
1 large garlic clove, finely minced

Whisk marinade ingredients together in a medium bowl and add cubed steak, being sure all is submerged. Set aside for 1 hour.

Meanwhile, heat half the olive oil and butter in a large stockpot. Add the chopped onion, carrot, and celery. Cook over medium to high heat until nicely golden, but not burned, about 5 minutes. Add mushrooms and continue cooking until they are just wilted, several more minutes. Remove and set aside. Wipe out any lingering bits of vegetable and add the remaining oil and butter.

Pat the steak cubes dry and flour them, shaking off excess. Brown in oil and butter over medium heat, being careful not to allow the flour to burn. Remove and set aside. Return cooked vegetables and mushrooms to the pot along with the sliced onions. Add 5 cups beef stock. Bring to a simmer and add salt, pepper, and bay leaf. Simmer for 15 minutes, skimming if necessary.

Add steak and simmer for another 10 minutes before adding escarole. You may add more stock here if you think the soup is too thick. Simmer just long enough for escarole to become tender. Do not overcook.

Correct seasoning if necessary.

Serves 6 to 8

Buttermilk Drop Biscuits

Here are my old standbys. Easy to make, they only have to be the proper consistency for success. And even if they are not, they will simply flatten out a little too much, but will still taste good.

    2 cups all-purpose flour
    1 teaspoon salt
    2 teaspoons baking powder
    ½ teaspoon baking soda
    6 tablespoons (¾ stick) chilled unsalted butter
    1½ cups buttermilk

Preheat oven to 450 degrees.

Sift flour, salt, baking powder, and soda together into a large bowl. Cut butter into chunks and then cut into flour with a pastry blender or 2 knives until butter is the size of large peas. Add buttermilk all at once, and stir just enough to mix.

Drop by tablespoonfuls onto an ungreased cookie sheet, leaving a few inches between. Bake until golden brown, about 12 to 15 minutes.

Makes 18 biscuits

Pear Pudding Cake

Delicious, and as easy as the biscuits to make.

    1 cup sugar
    6 tablespoons all-purpose flour
    1½ teaspoons baking powder
      Pinch of salt
    2 eggs, lightly beaten
    1 tablespoon bourbon

    1 tablespoon grated lemon rind
    1 cup coarsely chopped walnuts
    1 cup peeled and coarsely diced firm pear
      Vanilla Sauce (page 138) or vanilla ice cream

Garnish
    Pear slices
    Lemon juice
    Lemon rind or strips

Preheat oven to 350 degrees. Generously butter an 8-inch square baking dish.

Sift together the sugar, flour, baking powder, and salt. Add the eggs and beat for several minutes, until thoroughly mixed. Stir in the bourbon and lemon rind, mixing well again. Fold in nuts and pear. Pour into baking dish and bake until puffy and brown, about 30 to 35 minutes.

Serve with Vanilla Sauce or vanilla ice cream, garnished with a few slices of fresh pear bathed in fresh lemon juice and topped with a bit of lemon rind or a few lemon strips if you like.

Serves 6

Here's How

This menu is not particularly "do-aheadable," but even so it is comparatively uncomplicated to prepare and shouldn't be a problem if you can get started several hours before you want to serve the meal.

Set the steak to marinating, then prepare the vegetables and mushrooms for the soup. Set aside. Sift the dry ingredients for the biscuits and cut in the butter. Cover and stash in the refrigerator. The biscuits will then only take a minute later to stir up with the buttermilk and can go into the oven as you start eating the first course. (Do not add the buttermilk until you are ready to bake the biscuits.) And speaking of that, timing is more or less geared to when the potatoes are due to come out of the oven, since they should be served hot.

Make the dessert to bake along with the potatoes if you have 2 ovens, or earlier in the afternoon if you don't. Ideally, it is served warm, but this is not strictly necessary.

Duck, Turnip, and Squash Soup Dinner

Of course the first thing I thought of when duck soup crossed my mind was the Marx Brothers movie of the same name. You'll probably be relieved to know that this is as far as the comparison goes. Duck soup is no joke. The marinated duck produces a delicious stock to which you can add any combination of vegetables to make whatever variations of this dish you might like. The only caution I give is not to overwhelm the taste of the stock with vegetables whose flavors are too competitive.

To accompany the soup are bacon-walnut muffins that include a lot of sage.

The first course is an easy baked egg dish, and the dessert is a marvelous variation on the classic baked "crumble," here calling for citrus fruit and pineapple.

Menu

Baked Browned Butter Eggs
DUCK, TURNIP, AND SQUASH SOUP
Bacon-Walnut Muffins
Ambrosia Crumble
Wine
Coffee

Above: Duck, Turnip, and Squash Soup. *Far left:*
Baked Browned Butter Eggs. *Left:* Ambrosia
Crumble.

Duck, Turnip, and Squash Soup Dinner

Baked Browned Butter Eggs

These baked eggs would obviously make a very good nucleus around which to build a party breakfast. Just add the usual bacon, sausages, and a salad.

    6 tablespoons thinly sliced green onions
    6 tablespoons (¾ stick) unsalted butter, melted and browned
    6 teaspoons balsamic vinegar
    6 eggs
    ½ teaspoon salt or to taste
      Freshly ground black pepper

Preheat oven to 400 degrees.

Divide the onions, butter, and vinegar among 6 small ramekins. Drop an egg in each. Add salt and pepper.

Bake on a cookie sheet for 9 to 10 minutes, depending on how firm you like the yolk.

To serve, turn out eggs onto a round or square of toast, letting the juice be absorbed.

Serves 6

Duck, Turnip, and Squash Soup

The important thing to remember when preparing this soup—or any soup which includes assorted vegetables—is not to overcook them. This mistake is best avoided by allowing the vegetables to complete their cooking by retained heat. When they are almost tender, the soup is allowed to sit off the heat for up to 30 minutes before it is served.

Finishing the soup by this method will guarantee not only that the vegetables will retain their individual flavors and texture but that the soup will be at the proper temperature.

    1 5-pound duck
    1 large bay leaf
    1 large onion, peeled and cut in half
    1 large carrot, unpeeled and broken in half
    3 large ribs celery (with tops), broken into large pieces
    1 teaspoon dried thyme
    2 teaspoons salt, or more to taste

    1 teaspoon black pepper
    2 teaspoons balsamic vinegar
    1 tablespoon tomato paste
    2 generous cups sliced leeks (¼-inch rounds of white part only)
    1 cup peeled and cubed turnips
    2 cups peeled and cubed butternut squash
    2 cups peeled and cubed potato

Marinade
    1 teaspoon dried thyme
    2 large bay leaves
    12 juniper berries
    1 tablespoon salt
    2 teaspoons black pepper
      Large garlic clove
    1 tablespoon balsamic vinegar

Put the ingredients for the marinade in a food processor and purée to a paste. Rub duck inside and out with it and cover tightly. Marinate duck overnight.

The next day, preheat oven to 325 degrees.

Drain and pat duck dry. Split down the back and cut each half in two. Place in a roasting pan with a rack. Roast in a 325-degree oven for 1 hour. Turn pieces and roast for another hour.

Place roasted duck in a deep pot and cover with about 2 quarts of cold water. Add bay leaf, onion, carrot, and celery. Bring to a simmer and allow to cook very slowly for 1 hour or more until the meat is coming off the bone. Pour the fat out of the roasting pan and ladle a cup or so of the liquid from the pot into the pan. Place over low heat and scrape browned bits from the bottom of the pan, dissolving them where you can. Pour this back into the soup pot. Remove duck, and when cool, remove meat, dice, and reserve. Strain stock and discard vegetables, along with the bones and skin. Either degrease the stock or refrigerate overnight and lift congealed fat off the top before going on with the soup.

Measure out 8 cups of degreased stock. Refrigerate any leftover for another soup. Add the thyme, salt, pepper, and vinegar. Dissolve tomato paste in a cup of the heated pot liquid and add. Bring to a simmer. Add leeks and bring to a boil. Simmer for 10 minutes, then add all the other vegetables. Simmer 5 minutes more, and add duck meat, skimming if necessary. Simmer another 3 minutes before testing vegetables for doneness. They should be almost fork-tender. Turn off heat and allow to rest for up to 30 minutes before serving. Correct seasoning if necessary.

Serves 6 to 8

Bacon-Walnut Muffins

Substitute any nut here for the walnuts if you like. However, the slightly bitter taste of walnuts seems to blend with the other ingredients very well.

The amount of sage in these muffins gives them a very strong flavor, so if sage is not a favorite of yours by all means reduce the amount to suit your tastes.

  2 cups all-purpose flour
  3 teaspoons baking powder
  ½ teaspoon baking soda
  2 tablespoons ground sage
  ½ teaspoon white pepper
     Pinch of cayenne (ground red) pepper
  1 cup milk
  2 eggs
  ½ cup safflower oil
  1 cup crumbled or cubed crisp-fried thick bacon
  1 cup coarsely chopped walnuts

Preheat oven to 400 degrees. Generously grease 12 medium muffin cups.

Sift together the flour, baking powder, baking soda, sage, white pepper, and cayenne into a large bowl. Lightly beat together the milk, eggs, and oil. Combine with the dry ingredients; do not overmix. Stir in bacon and walnuts. Fill cups about three-fourths full and bake until golden, approximately 20 minutes.

Makes 12 muffins

Ambrosia Crumble

This particular crumble is a good one to remember. Its especially refreshing flavor provides a satisfying finish to almost any meal.

  ½ large ripe pineapple, peeled, cored, and cut into
     ½-inch cubes
  3 large seedless oranges, peeled (with white pith
     cut off) and sectioned
  3 ripe bananas, cut into 1-inch pieces
  1 cup shredded unsweetened coconut, fresh or
     canned
  3 tablespoons fresh lemon juice
  ¾ cup granulated sugar
  1 cup all-purpose flour
  ½ cup light brown sugar, tightly packed
  ½ cup (1 stick) unsalted butter, softened
     Vanilla ice cream or Vanilla Sauce (page 138)

Preheat oven to 350 degrees. Generously butter an 8-inch square or oval pan.

Toss fruit and ½ cup of the coconut with the lemon juice and heap into the buttered dish. Spread ¼ cup of the granulated sugar over all.

Mix remaining dry ingredients in a bowl. Then, using your fingers, rub in the butter to make a crumbly mixture. Pat onto the fruit.

Bake until top begins to turn golden, about 45 minutes.

Serve with vanilla ice cream or Vanilla Sauce.

Serves 6 to 8

Here's How

The first thing you should prepare is the duck stock. This can be done several days in advance. Other than that, this is not a particularly do-ahead-able meal. That's not to say this one is difficult; it just requires you to get all the chopping and other prepping done so it can run smoothly. For instance, make the dessert so it will come out of the oven just before your guests are due to arrive. Have the muffin ingredients ready to stir up (this is very easy) so they can bake while the soup goes through its final 30-minute resting period before being served. The muffins should go in just after the eggs come out; this means you will have to jump up from the table to take the muffins out of the oven during the first course, but that will only take a minute. Better this than having them made too far in advance.

However, if you do want to do them ahead, pop the precooked muffins in the still-warm oven with the door ajar when you serve the first course. A good compromise.

Gumbo Dinner

When I was planning the soups for this book, I decided not to include recipes for classic soups. I assumed nobody needed another recipe for vichyssoise, for instance, although I didn't rule out variations on the classics. The exception to my self-imposed limitation is the soup in this menu: gumbo. I allowed gumbo because it is the soup, above all others, that I was brought up on.

But to take away the curse of including it against my own rule, I have put it in another context. I start the meal with a vaguely Italian first course and finish with a rather tart dessert, in place of the more typical Southern beginning and ending to a gumbo meal.

The fried bread is good with any hearty soup.

Menu

Rustic Zucchini Tart
GUMBO
Deep-Fried Scallion Bread
Cranberry-Pear Sorbet
Wine
Coffee

Opposite: Gumbo with white rice and Deep-Fried Scallion Bread. Above: Rustic Zucchini Tart. Below: Cranberry-Pear Sorbet.

Gumbo Dinner

Rustic Zucchini Tart

"Rustic" means to me that you don't have to fuss too much with the shape and finishing of the pastry. This suits me just fine.

Pastry

¾ cup all-purpose flour
1 teaspoon dried thyme
¼ teaspoon black pepper
½ teaspoon salt
3 tablespoons chilled unsalted butter, cut into bits
1 tablespoon chilled solid vegetable shortening
1 tablespoon ice water

Filling

3 tablespoons unsalted butter
1 teaspoon dried basil
2 cups sliced onions
1 tablespoon minced garlic
2½ cups shredded zucchini
1 cup grated mozzarella cheese

To make the pastry, mix the flour, thyme, black pepper, and salt in a bowl. Cut in the butter and shortening with 2 knives or a pastry blender. Stir in water to make a ball. Flatten dough between 2 sheets of wax paper and refrigerate.

Preheat oven to 400 degrees.

Roll out the dough into a rough circle about 12 inches in diameter. Place circle on a cookie sheet and crimp the edges. Prick with the tines of a fork and bake until golden brown, about 15 minutes. Remove from oven and turn temperature to 350 degrees.

To make the filling, heat the butter over medium heat, stir in the basil, and then add the onions and garlic. Sauté until wilted, about 5 minutes. Add the zucchini and sauté until some of the liquid evaporates, another 5 minutes.

Spread the cheese evenly over pastry and top with the zucchini mixture. Smooth over.

Bake until well heated and cheese has melted, about 15 minutes.

Serves 6

Gumbo

There are basically two methods of making gumbo; they both include that key ingredient, roux, but the amount of roux and the use of a stock instead of water makes the difference. My father used quite a lot of roux for his soup, which is the way in the recipe that follows. To it may be added either chicken, duck, or seafood—or a combination of all of them.

For a less thick soup, the roux is made from only 2 tablespoons each of flour and oil, and fish stock is used instead of plain water. Ham or sausage is often a part of this version, as well as canned peeled tomatoes. Once you understand the basic taste of gumbo, you can make any variation you like.

1 cup safflower oil
1 cup coarsely chopped onions
1 cup coarsely chopped celery, including tops
¾ cup coarsely chopped green peppers
4 large garlic cloves, minced
¼ cup chopped fresh parsley
2 quarts water or Fish Stock (page 3)
¾ cup all-purpose flour
   Salt
   Black pepper
   Cayenne (ground red) pepper
   Worcestershire sauce (optional)
1 pound okra, tops and stems removed, cut into rings
1 pound peeled shrimp, or more to taste
1 pint shucked oysters and their liquid, or more to taste
   Boiled white rice
   Chopped green onions, with some tops

Place ¼ cup of the oil in a deep, heavy pot; when hot, add onions, celery, and green peppers. Sauté until wilted and starting to brown. Add garlic and parsley. Set aside.

Have the water heating while, in a heavy skillet, you mix the balance of the oil and the flour. Using the reverse side of a flat-end spatula (or pancake turner), keep the mixture moving as it begins to brown, scraping from the bottom. This is not a difficult process, but when the roux begins to brown it will do so very quickly and will continue to darken off the heat, so it is necessary to continue scraping. You want the roux to be a very dark brown. When the proper color is reached, add 1 cup of the heated water, stirring constantly. Pour this paste into the pot with the vegetables and add the balance of the water. Add salt, peppers, and optional Worcestershire sauce to taste. This should be very spicy and hot with pepper. Simmer for about 45 minutes. At the end of this cooking time, the oil will begin to rise to the top. Carefully skim it off and discard. Add more water if the mixture has become too thick, but this version of gumbo should be a bit thicker than the kind made with less roux. The soup may be put aside at this point.

To serve, add okra and cook until just tender, 5 or 10 minutes. Add seafood; cook until shrimp turns pink, another 5 to 10 minutes. Serve over rice, topped with chopped green onions over all.

Serves 6 to 8

Variation: To make chicken gumbo, generously salt and pepper a 4- to 5-pound chicken cut into serving pieces, and brown in safflower oil. Use the pot in which you intend to sauté the vegetables. Remove and reserve the chicken and continue with the recipe, adding the chicken when you start simmering the roux-vegetable-water mixture. Continue simmering until the chicken falls off the bones (bones and skin can be removed and discarded). Okra should be added at the end of the cooking time, but shrimp, oysters, and cooked crabs are optional. Serve as above.

Deep-Fried Scallion Bread

The only thing to remember about breads of this sort is that they toughen up as they stand, so plan to serve this hot.

   10 ounces (2 cups) all-purpose flour
    1 teaspoon salt
    1 teaspoon black pepper
    1 cup boiling water
    1 cup chopped green onions, including some tops
      Safflower oil for frying

Place flour, salt, and pepper in a food processor with a metal blade. Turn on machine and pour boiling water through the top in a steady stream. Continue to process for about another minute. The dough should be shiny and elastic. Wrap tightly in plastic wrap and allow to rest at room temperature for about 30 minutes.

Meanwhile, sauté green onions in a tablespoon of oil until they are wilted, about 5 minutes.

Turn dough out onto a floured surface and roll out with a floured pin into a rectangle approximately 14 × 16 inches. Spoon green onions evenly over dough and roll up jelly-roll fashion. Cut into 12 rounds and flatten each with the heel of the hand. (These can be refrigerated at this point to be fried later.)

Heat an inch of safflower oil in a heavy skillet until it is very hot but not smoking and fry each round until golden. Turn once. These cook very quickly, so be careful not to burn them.

Makes 12 puffs

Cranberry-Pear Sorbet

This is rather tart, so if you have a sweet tooth, add more sugar, tasting as you go along.

   ⅔ cup sugar
   ⅔ cup water
    3 cups fresh or frozen cranberries, puréed
    2 ripe pears, peeled, cored, and puréed
      Zest of 2 oranges
    2 tablespoons kirsch
    1 egg white

Combine sugar and water in a small saucepan and bring to a boil, stirring. When sugar is dissolved, allow to cool, then chill.

Mix chilled syrup, cranberries, pears, orange zest, and kirsch. Blend well. Freeze until mushy in an ice-cream machine or in metal ice trays.

Place slush in a food processor with the egg white. Process until smooth and fluffy. Refreeze in the ice-cream machine and refrigerate at least 1 hour before serving.

Makes 1 quart

Here's How

Make the gumbo up to the point of adding the seafood. You can put this in while you are finishing your first course. The rice can be cooked ahead because the soup heats it when it is served.

Of course, the sorbet may be made anytime. This leaves only the bread, which goes into the oven to stay warm when the tart comes out. Make the tart dough in advance, as well as the topping, so that it will just have to be assembled and quickly baked at the last minute—like a pizza.

Above: Lamb, Pumpkin, and Lima Bean Soup with Salt Wafers. *Left:* Baked Winter Fruit. *Right:* Mandich Oysters.

Lamb, Pumpkin, and Lima Bean Soup Dinner

This soup is one of the last recipes I came up with, and the making of it happened to coincide with the pumpkin season. So much for planning ahead.

It contains frozen lima beans, which to my way of thinking are almost every bit as good as fresh, one of the few frozen vegetables I can say that about. Limas are simply too much trouble for me to shell. Anyway, I had almost forgotten how really delightful their flavor can be in a soup.

The secret in this recipe is the lift that the caramelized sugar gives it.

An easy salt cracker accompanies the soup.

The first course is fried oysters, which always remind me of New Orleans. The dessert is three-nut cookies and nourishing baked fruit.

All in all, a nice menu to slip you into fall.

Menu

Mandich Oysters
LAMB, PUMPKIN, AND LIMA BEAN SOUP
Salt Wafers
Baked Winter Fruit
Three-Nut Cookies
Wine
Coffee

Lamb, Pumpkin, and Lima Bean Soup Dinner

Mandich Oysters

These oysters get their name from Mandich Restaurant in New Orleans, where they are a house specialty. The dish is the inspiration of Joel English, who together with her husband Lloyd, runs the popular family-style place out near fabled Desire Street in the Crescent City.

¼ cup olive oil
¾ cup safflower oil
3 tablespoons coarsely chopped garlic
¼ cup minced green onions
¾ teaspoon salt
⅛ teaspoon black pepper
2 tablespoons dry sherry
1 quart vegetable oil for deep-frying
2 eggs
1 cup all-purpose flour
1 tablespoon paprika
2 to 3 dozen medium oysters, shucked, with deeper half of the shell reserved
2 tablespoons chopped fresh parsley

Garnish
 Lemon wedges

Place olive and safflower oils in a medium saucepan and add garlic, green onions, salt, and pepper. Simmer very gently or until garlic is tender but not browned, about 30 minutes. Off the heat, stir in sherry and set aside.
 Heat the vegetable oil to 425 degrees in a deep pot.
 While the oil is heating, beat eggs in a small bowl. In a shallow dish combine flour and paprika. Drain oysters and, one at the time, dip them first in flour, then in the egg (allow excess to drain off), and then dredge in flour mixture again. Shake off excess flour. Working in batches, fry the oysters until crisp, about 15 to 20 seconds.
 Place 2 oysters (or more) in each reserved half shell and spoon about 1 teaspoon of the sauce over each. Sprinkle with parsley and garnish with lemon.

Serves 6 generously

Lamb, Pumpkin, and Lima Bean Soup

Whenever I make lamb soups, I always use lamb from the leg. It tends not to have so much fat, which I don't like at all.
 If pumpkins are not in season, use a hard winter squash in its place.

¼ cup safflower oil
1½ pounds lamb cut from the leg, trimmed and cut into 1-inch cubes
3 tablespoons unsalted butter
2 cups coarsely chopped onions
2 tablespoons sugar
2 quarts Beef Stock (page 75), heated
1 cup small dried lima beans, soaked overnight or use the Quick-Soak Method (page 22)
1 teaspoon dried thyme
1 bay leaf
1½ teaspoons salt
½ teaspoon black pepper
2 cups cubed pumpkin, in ½-inch dice

Garnish
 Green onion strips

Heat oil in a deep pot and quickly sear the meat until it is completely brown. Remove with a slotted spoon and set aside. Pour out oil and add butter. Sauté onions until wilted, about 5 minutes, then sprinkle with sugar and stir. Continue to cook until the sugar begins to turn golden and caramelize. Add the stock and stir to melt the sugar.
 Add lima beans, thyme, bay leaf, salt, pepper, and lamb. Bring to a boil and then turn back to a simmer. Cook for about 20 to 25 minutes, skimming very often, until beans and meat are almost tender.
 Stir in pumpkin and cook until just tender, about 8 to 10 minutes. Do not overcook the pumpkin or it will lose its flavor and texture. Correct seasoning if necessary.
 Serve garnished with thin strips of green onion.

Serves 6 to 8

Salt Wafers

These crisp little squares were inspired by Nathalie Dupree's "Brittlebread."

Many of you know Ms. Dupree as the hostess of the nationally broadcast PBS cooking show that emanates from Atlanta.

1¾ cups all-purpose flour
1 cup whole wheat flour
2 tablespoons sugar
¾ teaspoon salt
¼ teaspoon black pepper
½ teaspoon baking soda
½ cup (1 stick) unsalted butter
1 cup low-fat sour cream
   Kosher (coarse) salt for topping

Preheat oven to 400 degrees.

Sift together the flours, sugar, salt, pepper, and baking soda. Cut in the butter with a pastry blender or 2 knives. Beat in the sour cream.

Roll out dough until paper-thin on a floured surface. Cut into saltine-size (2-inch) squares and place on 2 ungreased cookie sheets. Sprinkle each with salt.

Bake for approximately 7 minutes and then turn off heat. Allow to crisp as the oven cools.

Makes about 60 wafers

Baked Winter Fruit

This comes out with the figs all plumped up and the apples still having a little crunch.

½ pound dried figs
1 large lemon, cut in half, with one half juiced and the other cut into thin rings and seeded
1½ firm pears, peeled, cored, and quartered
⅓ cup sugar
1 pound apples, peeled, cored, and cut in eighths

Preheat oven to 350 degrees. Butter a deep 6-cup casserole.

Place figs on the bottom of the casserole, sprinkle with half the lemon juice, and scatter half the lemon slices over. Put the pears on top of this and sprinkle with half the sugar, remaining lemon juice, and the balance of the lemon slices. Top with the apples and sprinkle with the balance of the sugar.

Bake, uncovered, for about 30 minutes. Cover loosely with foil and turn off oven. Leave in oven for another hour. The apples should retain some of their texture, and the pears will be soft.

Serves 6

Three-Nut Cookies

1½ cups all-purpose flour
1 teaspoon cream of tartar
½ teaspoon baking soda
   Pinch of salt
½ cup (1 stick) unsalted butter, softened
¾ cup sugar
1 egg
1½ cups very coarsely chopped macadamia nuts
1 cup slivered almonds
1 cup finely grated pecans
½ cup light brown sugar, tightly packed
1 tablespoon ground cinnamon

Preheat oven to 400 degrees. Grease 2 cookie sheets.

Sift together the flour, cream of tartar, baking soda, and salt. Set aside.

In a large bowl, cream the butter and sugar until fluffy. Beat in the egg. Add the dry ingredients to the wet mixture in 2 parts. Mix well. Stir in the macadamia nuts and almonds.

Thoroughly mix pecans, brown sugar, and cinnamon.

Pinch off walnut-size pieces of dough and form into balls. Roll each ball in the pecan-sugar mixture and place on the cookie sheet about 2 inches apart. Do not flatten.

Bake until browned, about 10 minutes.

Makes approximately 2 dozen cookies

Here's How

Make the soup the day before, up to the point of adding the beans and pumpkin. Finish it off just before starting the oysters. You don't want to overwhelm the flavor and texture of the pumpkin, so don't let the soup sit too long after it is cooked.

Everything else should be ready when you start the oysters, including their sauce.

Make the salt wafers in the afternoon, and put the dessert in to bake just before your guests are due to arrive so it will still be warm when served.

Lentil, Fennel, and Cress Soup Dinner

Left: Lentil, Fennel, and Cress Soup with Scotch Unkneaded Bread. Above: Lobster with Tarragon Mayonnaise. Below: Plum Sorbet.

Lentil, Fennel, and Cress Soup Dinner

Lentils are about my favorite dried bean. I am constantly amazed at how flexible they are and how adaptable their flavor is to other foods. Here, for instance, their natural nutty taste is enhanced by fennel and the pepper of watercress—all melded so you really can't distinguish one from the other. Delicious and warming, the soup is accompanied by a very easy to prepare Scotch bread.

To start the meal is the surprise of a small lobster salad. We all know it is popular in the summer, but why must lobster salad be eaten only then?

And finally there is the palate-cleansing finish of plum sorbet. Add a little sugar wafer here, if you like.

Menu

Lobster with Tarragon Mayonnaise
LENTIL, FENNEL, AND CRESS SOUP
Scotch Unkneaded Bread
Plum Sorbet
Wine
Coffee

Lobster with Tarragon Mayonnaise

The palate-teasing flavor of this salad is very dependent on fresh tarragon leaves—dried won't do. Luckily, fresh herbs may be grown on windowsills and now seem also to be available in specialty markets for most of the year.

The only problem with indoor cultivation of herbs is that their flavor seems to be fainter, so you may want to add extra leaves if you have grown your own tarragon inside.

- 3 generous cups cooked lobster meat, cut into large cubes
- 1 tablespoon minced shallots
- 1 generous tablespoon snipped fresh tarragon leaves
  Zest of 1 lemon
- 2 tablespoons tarragon vinegar
- 3 tablespoons crème fraîche
- ½ cup Homemade Mayonnaise (page 6)
  Salt and pepper to taste

Garnish
- Bibb lettuce leaves
- Lemon wedges
- 4 hard-boiled eggs, quartered

Place lobster, shallots, tarragon, lemon zest, and tarragon vinegar in a large bowl and toss. Allow to marinate briefly. Mix crème fraîche and mayonnaise and fold into the salad. Correct seasoning.

Serve garnished with bibb lettuce leaves, lemon wedges, and quartered hard-boiled eggs, if desired.

Serves 6

Lentil, Fennel, and Cress Soup

This soup freezes fairly well because it does not depend so much on texture as it does on overall flavor.

- 3 tablespoons olive oil
- 1 cup coarsely chopped fennel (tender parts only and no tops)
- ¾ cup coarsely chopped onions
- ½ cup coarsely chopped celery
- ¼ cup finely chopped carrot
  Generous ¼ cup finely chopped red bell pepper
- 1 bunch watercress (about ½ pound), large stems removed
- 1 medium garlic clove, minced
- 1½ cups brown lentils, picked over, soaked for several hours, and drained
- 5 to 6 cups heated rich Chicken Stock (page 74)
  Scant ⅛ teaspoon dried thyme
- ¼ teaspoon salt, or to taste
- ¼ teaspoon black pepper, or to taste
- 1 medium bay leaf
- 4 dashes Tabasco
- 2 tablespoons (¼ stick) unsalted butter (optional)

Garnish
- Additional watercress sprigs

Place olive oil in a deep pot and add fennel, onions, celery, carrot, and red pepper. Sauté until it starts to brown and turn soft, a few minutes. Add watercress and cook until just wilted, a few more minutes. Add garlic, lentils, and about 4 cups of the stock. Bring to a simmer and add thyme, salt, pepper, bay leaf, and Tabasco. Cook over very low heat for about 20 minutes, until lentils are tender and falling apart, adding a bit more stock if necessary.

Place soup in a food processor and purée. Return to pot and add balance of the stock and heat thoroughly. I prefer this soup rather thick, but it can be diluted with additional stock if you like. Stir in optional butter.

Serve with a sprig of watercress on top.

Serves 6 to 8

Scotch Unkneaded Bread

Margaret Brown, a British friend of mine, gave me this recipe. It is an easy way to make bread because it requires no kneading and not much rising time. It's dense and very good toasted.

> ½ pound (approximately 1¾ cups) whole wheat flour
> ½ pound (approximately 1¾ cups) all-purpose flour
> 2 teaspoons salt
> 2 packages active dry yeast
> 1 tablespoon sugar
> 2 tablespoons dark molasses
> 1 cup hot water
> ½ cup chopped walnuts

Sift flours, salt, yeast, and sugar together. Dissolve molasses in the hot water and stir into the flour mixture. Add walnuts and mix well to form a ball. Put in a greased bowl, lightly covered with a tea towel, and place in a warm, draft-free spot. Allow to rise to about half again its original bulk, approximately 45 minutes.

Preheat oven to 400 degrees. Grease an 8 x 4-inch loaf pan.

Turn into loaf pan and bake for about 35 minutes. Brush with water and bake until set and very lightly golden, another 5 minutes.

Makes 1 loaf

Plum Sorbet

Strangely enough, I had never thought of making sorbet from plums until a friend brought me a big basket of them. So many, in fact, I had to think of some way to use them all.

This is the happy result.

> 2 cups water
> ⅓ cup sugar
> 1 tablespoon fresh lemon juice
> 2 pounds dark plums, halved, with pits removed

Combine water, sugar, and lemon juice in a saucepan and heat. Add plums and bring to a simmer over medium heat. Simmer, skimming if necessary, for 8 to 10 minutes. Pour the whole mixture into a food processor and purée. Allow to cool, then freeze in an ice-cream maker according to the manufacturer's directions.

Makes about 1½ pints

Here's How

You know I often talk about preparing parts of the meal in advance, but I don't know if I have ever made clear how I actually do this myself. I find it relaxing to cook when I take a break from some other chores—like writing.

For instance, unless I were on a tight schedule, I would probably do the above menu over a period of several days. I'd likely start with the soup or the bread, putting the beans to soak and then readying the bread up to the point at which it must be set aside to rise. I'd then go on about my business until it was time to get back into the kitchen to finish them both. Under ideal circumstances that would be enough for one day, and I'd leave steaming the lobsters and making the sorbet for the next.

Lobster meat tends to toughen up in the refrigerator if it is left too long, so I would certainly leave the assembling of the salad to the last few minutes before it is served. However, all the chopping and gathering of ingredients would be done beforehand.

Don't forget to check the sorbet if it is in the freezer. If it is a solid block of ice, transfer the mixture to the refrigerator when you sit down to eat, to give it a chance to soften up a bit (do the same with ice cream that has gotten too hard).

Ossobuco Soup Dinner

I guess you could call this a sort of Americanized Italian meal. The Ossobuco turned into a soup is a delectable variation of a long-standing favorite, and the first course is something right out of Italy except the greens, which in this case are that old Southern standby, mustard greens. Along with the soup there are nut muffins and for dessert a smooth Vermont maple syrup flan with raspberries.

Incidentally, if the soup is served in a wide, flat soup bowl, this will make the veal easier to cut with a knife and fork—and also makes a very nice presentation.

Menu

Wilted Greens with Olive Oil and Lemon
OSSOBUCO SOUP
Nut Muffins
Maple Syrup Flan with Berries
Wine
Coffee

Left: Wilted Greens with Olive Oil and Lemon.
Above: Ossobuco Soup with Nut Muffins.
Opposite: Maple Syrup Flan with Berries.

Ossobuco
Soup Dinner

Wilted Greens with Olive Oil and Lemon

The cooking time here may vary somewhat depending on how mature the greens are. They should be cooked until tender.

Mustard greens, like their relatives collards and kale, are very sturdy vegetables and may be reheated without destroying their texture. Of the three, mustard greens are my favorite.

A substitute for mustard could be broccoli rabe or the old reliable spinach.

2 tablespoons mild olive oil
1 medium onion
2 small shallots
2 tablespoons Chicken Stock (page 74)
2 small garlic cloves, finely minced
2 pounds fresh mustard greens, washed, with large stems removed
2 teaspoons fresh lemon juice
½ teaspoon salt
¼ teaspoon freshly ground black pepper

Garnish
Lemon wedges
Green onions
Hard-boiled egg, grated

In a deep pot with a lid, heat olive oil and sauté onion and shallots until golden, about 10 minutes. Mix in chicken stock and garlic. Place washed greens on top. Cover and cook over medium heat for about 20 minutes. This will reduce considerably in volume, and greens should be turned several times during the cooking period. Sprinkle with the lemon juice, salt, and pepper. Toss.

Serve warm with extra olive oil on the side. Garnish with lemon wedges, green onions, and grated hard-boiled egg.

Serves 6

Ossobuco Soup

Obviously, this is a very hearty soup and should be served with a knife and fork as well as the soup spoon. If you think it would be easier to eat, you could cut each veal slice into bite-size pieces, but I prefer to serve it unsliced.

8 small, meaty slices veal shank, cut 1–1½ inches thick, with bone in (about 2½–3 pounds)
Salt
Freshly ground black pepper
Flour for dusting
¼ cup olive oil
¼ cup (½ stick) unsalted butter
1 medium onion, finely chopped
1 medium carrot, peeled and finely chopped
1 large rib celery, finely chopped
1½ cups dry light red wine
1 ½-inch-wide strip lemon rind
12 large pitted green olives
6 small fresh sage leaves (no stems)
2 teaspoons fresh rosemary leaves
1 small garlic clove
2 tablespoons drained capers
5¾ cups Chicken Stock (page 74) or substitute veal
¾ cup basmati rice (or long-grain)

Dry veal shank slices, salt lightly, and dust generously with pepper. Flour both sides, shaking off excess. Heat half the oil and butter in a deep, heavy pot and brown the floured ends, being careful not to burn the butter. Do this in batches. Set meat aside.

Meanwhile, heat the balance of the oil and butter in a large skillet and sauté the onion, carrot, and celery until wilted, about 5 minutes. Add ¾ cup of the red wine and boil over medium heat until reduced to a few table-spoons, 6 to 8 minutes. Set aside.

Mince together the lemon rind, olives, sage leaves, rosemary leaves, garlic, and capers. Pour oil and butter from the pot in which veal was browned. Return veal to the pot and add the sautéed vegetables with the reduced wine and minced ingredients. Pour in the balance of the red wine plus ¾ cup of the chicken or veal stock. Bring to a boil and turn back to a simmer. Cover tightly and cook for 40 minutes.

Add the balance of the veal or chicken stock and continue to simmer, uncovered, until veal is fork-tender, about another hour. Skim off oil and fat as it rises.

To serve, cook rice in well-salted water, then drain. Place several generous spoonfuls of rice in a flat-bottom soup bowl and top with a veal slice. Pour soup over all.

Serves 6 to 8

Nut Muffins

Notice that I specify toasted nuts in this recipe. This is something that I almost always do when I'm adding nuts to a dish. I think toasting vastly improves their flavor.

¾ cup coarse whole wheat flour
½ cup bran flakes
1¼ teaspoons baking powder
½ teaspoon salt
½ cup milk
1 egg
1 tablespoon dark molasses
2 tablespoons (¼ stick) unsalted butter, melted
1 cup toasted nut meats

Preheat oven to 425 degrees. Grease a 12-cup muffin pan (2-inch cups) or coat cups with vegetable cooking spray.

In a large bowl, mix the flour, bran flakes, baking powder, and salt. In a separate bowl, combine milk, egg, and molasses. Mix until molasses is dissolved. Pour into the dry mixture all at once and add the melted butter. Quickly stir just to combine; do not overmix. Batter should be lumpy. Stir in nuts. Divide among the muffin cups.

Bake until browned on top, about 15 to 17 minutes.

Allow to cool about a minute in the pan, then loosen edges and turn out.

Makes 12 muffins

Maple Syrup Flan with Berries

Obviously, any berry would be good with this flan, but the golden raspberries in the photograph just happened to be available in the market and were almost the same color as the finished flan.

1 cup pure maple syrup
2 cups milk
1 cup heavy cream
4 eggs, room temperature
1 egg yolk, room temperature
1 teaspoon vanilla extract
1 pint fresh raspberries or strawberries
2 tablespoons maple sugar or light brown sugar

Preheat oven to 300 degrees.

Heat ¾ cup of the syrup in a heavy saucepan until it starts to boil. Continue boiling over moderate heat, stirring occasionally, for 10 minutes. Remove from heat and stir briefly until the foam is dissolved. Pour into a 6-cup ring mold and quickly tilt (holding mold with a pot holder) to evenly coat the bottom of the mold.

In the same saucepan, combine the milk and cream. Bring slowly to a boil and stir to dissolve the syrup remaining in the pan. Meanwhile, beat the remaining ¼ cup of syrup with the eggs and egg yolk. Gradually whisk the hot milk and cream into the beaten eggs. Stir in the vanilla.

Strain the custard into the ring mold. Place the mold in a larger pan and add enough hot water to reach halfway up the mold.

Bake until set, about 50 minutes. Remove mold from the water bath and let cool. Refrigerate until chilled, about 1 hour.

To serve, run a knife around the edges of the mold and invert onto a serving plate with a lip. Toss the berries with the sugar and mound in the center of the ring—and around the outside if you have enough of them.

Serves 6

Note: Often when you turn out a flan some of the caramel remains in the pan. You might butter just the bottom of the pan to help prevent sticking. However, do not butter the pan on the sides, as the custard needs an ungreased surface to cling to.

Here's How

This is another do-ahead meal. Everything in the menu can be prepared in advance, although, as I always point out, muffins are so much better fresh from the oven. They are so easy to stir up that it is worth the small extra effort making them at the last minute requires.

When you make the soup ahead, put the veal slices in a separate container to store them so they don't have to be handled too much. To serve, let the slices come to room temperature, then pour a little of the hot soup over them a few minutes before transferring to the soup plates. This should be sufficient to warm them through, if the soup has been brought to a boil.

The greens are sturdy and can be reheated and then allowed to rest until ready to be served. Of course, the flan can be made a day ahead.

Above: Piperade Pie. Below: Fresh Figs Marinated in Lemon. Opposite: Sausage and White Bean Soup with Cottage Cheese Biscuits.

Sausage and White Bean Soup Dinner

Who doesn't like bean soup? It has got to be one of the best stick-to-your-ribs dishes going. And here is a version that I think has a very special flavor. It is topped with sausages. They are certainly not necessary to the success of the soup, however they *do* give it an added flavor lift. The cottage cheese biscuits served with the soup are a treat, too.

The first course is also a sturdy dish, a pie made of tomatoes, peppers, and eggs—among other things—with a cheese crust.

And dessert is marinated fruit. Of course, any sort of fruit would do if figs are too expensive or are simply not a special favorite of yours.

Sausage and White Bean Soup Dinner

Menu

Piperade Pie
SAUSAGE AND WHITE BEAN SOUP
Cottage Cheese Biscuits
Fresh Figs Marinated in Lemon
Wine
Coffee

Piperade Pie

Piperade is a tomatoey-eggy Basque dish that is very popular in France. As a pie it makes a very nice center course for a small winter luncheon with the addition of a green salad and dessert. Keep it in mind.

Crust

    1 cup all-purpose flour
      Pinch of salt
    ¼ cup (½ stick) unsalted butter, cut into bits and frozen
    2 tablespoons solid vegetable shortening, frozen
    1 cup grated cheddar cheese
    2 tablespoons ice water

Filling

    4½ tablespoons olive oil
    1¼ cups coarsely chopped red bell peppers
    ¾ cup coarsely chopped onions
    6 tablespoons coarsely chopped green onions, including some tops
    1 tablespoon minced garlic
    3 cups drained canned peeled tomatoes, coarsely chopped (or an equal amount of peeled and seeded fresh tomatoes)
    2 teaspoons dried basil, or 2 tablespoons coarsely chopped fresh
    1 tablespoon salt, or to taste
    1½ teaspoons black pepper
    6 dashes Tabasco
    3 tablespoons unsalted butter, melted
    6 eggs, lightly beaten

To make the crust, toss flour and salt together in a large bowl. Cut in butter, shortening, and cheese with 2 knives or a pastry blender until the mixture resembles coarse meal. Stir in water, mixing well but quickly. Form into a ball and flatten between 2 sheets of wax paper. Refrigerate for 30 minutes.

Preheat oven to 400 degrees.

Roll out the dough between the 2 sheets of wax paper (or on a lightly floured surface) and line a 10-inch pie pan, crimping the edges and pricking the bottom of the crust with the tines of a fork. Then line the pan with foil. Cover bottom with a layer of dried peas or pie weights. Bake for 15 minutes until the crust is set. Remove foil and weights. Bake another 10 minutes or until golden. Set aside.

Preheat oven to 350 degrees.

To make the filling, in a large skillet over medium heat, heat the olive oil and sauté the peppers, onions, and green onions until the vegetables are wilted, about 10 minutes. Stir in garlic. Add tomatoes, basil, salt, pepper, and Tabasco. Bring to a slow simmer and continue cooking to reduce the liquid, about another 10 minutes. Stir in melted butter, then mix in eggs.

Pour mixture into the baked pie shell and bake until filling is set, but not dry, about 30 minutes.

Allow to rest for a few minutes before slicing.

Serves 6 to 8

Sausage and White Bean Soup

You can use any sausage that appeals to you for this. And incidentally, this method of cooking sausage is a good one to know about—it's foolproof, and always improves the flavor of whatever sausage you are preparing.

    2 cups dried white (navy) beans
    8 cups Chicken Stock (page 74)
    1 large bay leaf
    ¼ teaspoon dried thyme
    ¼ cup olive oil
    1½ cups coarsely chopped onions
    ½ cup coarsely chopped celery
    2 large carrots, peeled and cut into rings
    ¼ large green bell pepper, coarsely chopped
    12 links pork sausage, (about 1–1¼ pounds)
    2 large garlic cloves, minced
    ¼ cup dry red wine

Pick over beans and soak overnight, or use the Quick-Soak Method on page 22. Drain and place beans, chicken stock, bay leaf, and thyme in a large pot. Bring to a simmer and continue to cook, skimming as necessary, until beans begin to get tender and fall apart, 1½ to 2 hours. Add another 2 cups of chicken stock, or to taste, if soup has reduced too much at the end of the cooking time.

Meanwhile, place olive oil in a large skillet and sauté all the vegetables except the garlic until they start to brown. Scrape into a food processor and purée. Reserve this purée and add to the beans for the last 30 minutes of their cooking time.

Place sausages in a cold skillet and cook over high heat for 6 minutes, turning often. Pour off the fat. Add the garlic and red wine. Simmer, covered, for another 15 minutes. Cut the sausages into rings and add to the soup. Degrease the pan with a few tablespoons of water or chicken stock, then add to soup.

Serves 6 to 8

Note: To cut down on the cooking time, substitute dried baby lima beans for the navy beans, since limas don't require more than about 45 minutes to cook.

Cottage Cheese Biscuits

This recipe makes a very soft and doughy biscuit, which is marvelous toasted.

> 2 cups all-purpose flour
> 1 teaspoon salt
> 2½ teaspoons baking powder
> 6 tablespoons (¾ stick) unsalted butter, chilled
> 1½ cups small-curd cottage cheese

Preheat oven to 450 degrees.

Sift the flour, salt, and baking powder into a large bowl. Cut the butter in with a pastry blender or 2 knives until it is the size of small peas. Stir in the cottage cheese all at once.

Drop by generous tablespoonfuls onto an ungreased cookie sheet. Bake until golden, about 15 minutes.

Makes approximately 18 biscuits

Fresh Figs Marinated in Lemon

It is important to prepare these well enough in advance to allow the flavors and texture to develop.

> 4 cups water
> 1 cup sugar
> ½ cup fresh lemon juice
> 2 lemons, cut into thick slices and seeds removed
> 12 large green figs, stems left on
> Devonshire cream or Vanilla Sauce (page 138)

Bring water, sugar, and lemon juice to a boil. Add lemon slices and simmer for 3 minutes.

Meanwhile, wash figs and place in a glass bowl. Pour hot liquid and lemons over all. Cover with a plate that fits inside the bowl to keep the figs submerged. Allow to cool, then cover with plastic wrap and refrigerate for several days.

Serve with Devonshire (clotted) cream or Vanilla Sauce.

Serves 6

Here's How

It may be my imagination, but I think this soup is better if you use the overnight soaking method for the beans instead of the quick-soak method. Anyway, make the soup a day or so in advance to allow the flavors to meld. The sausages can also be cooked ahead, but don't mix them in until the soup is reheated prior to serving. (Stir the wine-garlic-sausage cooking liquid in the soup while the liquid is hot.)

You can also make the pie crust a day ahead and have it ready to bake; ditto the filling, but without the eggs and butter, which should be added just before the final baking. However, the pie need not be just out of the oven for it to be good. As a matter of fact, it can be timed to finish baking just before the guests are due to arrive.

The biscuits must be served hot, or if made ahead, toasted. As I've said, the dessert is best if made in advance.

Left to right: Broccoli Rabe, Black-Eyed Pea, White Bean, and Sausage Soup; Chicken, Chard, Lettuce, and Two-Potato Soup; Ham, Mustard Green, Red Bean, and Sweet Potato Soup; Five Bean Soup.

VARIATIONS ON WINTER SOUP MEALS

Soups

Five Bean Soup

This meal is for those of you who like to have a real Tex/Mex fix. There are plenty of spices in the soup.

½ cup dried black beans
½ cup dried red kidney beans
½ cup dried white (navy) beans
½ cup dried black-eyed peas
½ cup dried baby lima beans
¾ pound andouille (spicy New Orleans) sausage
1 medium smoked ham hock (about 10 ounces)
4 cups water
1 large carrot, unpeeled, broken into several pieces
3 large ribs celery, broken into several large pieces
3 large sprigs parsley
1 very large onion (about ¾ pound), coarsely chopped
¼ cup olive oil
2 large garlic cloves, finely chopped
1 large bay leaf
2½ teaspoons salt
2 teaspoons paprika
2 teaspoons ground cumin
2 teaspoons chili powder
1 teaspoon black pepper
¼ teaspoon ground cinnamon
2 cups chopped canned whole tomatoes in paste
2 cups Beef Stock (page 75)
1 teaspoon red wine vinegar

Place all beans except baby limas in a bowl and cover with water. Soak overnight or use the Quick-Soak Method (see Note, page 22). Soak limas separately.

Cover sausage and ham hock with the water and bring to a boil. Add carrot, celery, and parsley. Turn back to just simmering and simmer for 1 hour, removing sausage after about 15 minutes. Set aside.

Sauté chopped onion in olive oil until wilted and brown, about 5 minutes. Add garlic and set aside.

Drain and degrease liquid in which sausage and hock were cooked. Discard vegetables and remove any meat from hock. Chop coarsely. Discard skin and bones.

Drain mixed beans and place in a large pot. Measure degreased liquid and add enough water to make 4 cups. Pour over beans and bring to a boil. Add onion-garlic mixture and turn heat back to a simmer. Add spices. Simmer until almost tender, about 1½ to 2 hours.

Add chopped tomatoes and beef stock to the pot. When simmering, add drained baby limas. Simmer until they are just cooked, about 30 minutes.

Cut sausage into ¼-inch rings. Add to soup along with ham and vinegar. Simmer another few minutes.

Serves 6 to 8

Ham, Mustard Green, Red Bean, and Sweet Potato Soup

Here is another soup which calls for an unusual green, mustard greens, arguably my favorite of them all. It combines perfectly with the taste of sweet potato.

1½ cups dried red kidney beans
4 pounds smoked ham hocks
3 quarts water
4 very large garlic cloves, crushed
1½ teaspoons freshly ground black pepper
1 teaspoon salt
4 large sprigs curly parsley
2 bay leaves
1½ teaspoons dried thyme
3 medium to large leeks, carefully cleaned and cut into rounds (white part only)
2 medium onions, cut into large rings
1 pound sweet potatoes, peeled and cubed
1½ pounds mustard greens, washed, stemmed, and torn into large pieces
½ cup or more cubed cooked ham (optional)

Place beans in a large pot and add enough water to cover by 1 inch. Bring rapidly to a boil and turn back to a slow boil. Cook for 2 minutes, then turn off heat. Cover and let stand for 1 hour. Or cover red beans with cold water and allow to soak overnight.

Meanwhile, place ham hocks in a large stockpot and cover with water. Bring to a boil and turn back to a simmer. Cook, partially covered, for about 2 hours. Skim as necessary. Remove hocks and allow to cool.

Degrease liquid in the stockpot. Drain and add beans. Bring to a simmer and add garlic and seasonings. Simmer until just tender, 1 to 1½ hours.

While beans are cooking, remove meat from hocks and discard skin and bones. Chop coarsely and add to beans when they are done.

Bring soup back to a simmer and add all other vegetables except mustard greens. Cook, barely simmering, for another 15 minutes. Correct seasoning if necessary. Add greens and cook until just tender, 10 minutes or so. Do not overcook.

Add optional ham at this point and allow to sit in the pot for 15 minutes before serving. You can add a couple more cups of hot water if mixture is too thick. However, it should be almost like a vegetable stew.

Serves 8

Broccoli Rabe, Black-Eyed Pea, White Bean, and Sausage Soup

As recently as five years ago, broccoli rabe was not generally available in markets around here except for specialty shops. Happily, now it is cropping up everyplace. This soup is a small celebration of the emergence of this vegetable (which the Italians have enjoyed for ages.)

 1 cup dried black-eyed peas, rinsed and picked over to remove any grit
 1 cup dried white (navy) beans, rinsed and picked over to remove any grit
 8 cups Chicken Stock (page 74)
 4 medium onions, chopped
 2 large garlic gloves, crushed
 2 bay leaves
 ½ teaspoon dried thyme
 ½ teaspoon freshly ground black pepper
1½ tablespoons olive oil
 1 pound bulk breakfast sausage, formed into 1-inch balls
 ½ pound broccoli rabe, tough stems removed and remainder chopped
  Salt to taste

Soak peas and beans in water using the Quick-Soak Method (see Note, page 22).

Drain peas and beans and return to the pot. Add chicken stock and bring to a boil over moderate heat. Add onions, garlic, bay leaves, thyme, and pepper. Simmer until beans are tender, skimming as necessary; this will take about 30 to 60 minutes or more.

Meanwhile, heat ½ tablespoon of olive oil in a large skillet over moderate heat. Add the sausage balls and cook, turning, until browned all over and cooked through, about 10 minutes. Drain on paper towels.

When beans are tender, add broccoli rabe and return to a simmer. Continue simmering until rabe is tender, skimming if necessary. Stir in remaining olive oil and sausage balls. Season with salt if necessary. Heat through, then let stand for 15 minutes before serving.

Serves 6 to 8

Chicken, Chard, Lettuce, and Two-Potato Soup

Chard is too often neglected in soups—it adds quite a distinctive flavor.

 1 chicken, about 4½ to 5 pounds
 7 large ribs celery with leaves, chopped
2½ quarts water
1½ pounds Swiss chard
 ¼ cup (½ stick) unsalted butter
 ¾ cup coarsely chopped green onions
 2 large baking potatoes, peeled and cubed
 1 small head Boston lettuce
 1 large sweet potato, peeled and cubed
 1 tablespoon salt
 ¾ teaspoon ground coriander
 ½ teaspoon freshly ground black pepper
 ⅛ teaspoon cayenne (ground red) pepper

Stuff chicken with 3 cups of celery and place it with balance of celery in a stockpot. Add the water to cover. Bring to a boil over high heat; reduce to moderately low. Simmer, partially covered, until tender, about 1½ hours. Remove from heat and allow to cool.

When chicken has cooled, remove meat and coarsely chop. Set aside (covered). Discard skin. Return bones and all celery to liquid in pot. Simmer, uncovered, for 1 hour, or until reduced to 8 cups. Strain and skim off fat. Let cool, then refrigerate until ready to use.

Strip leaves from chard and set aside; chop stems into ½-inch pieces. Melt butter in stockpot; add green onions. Cook over low heat, uncovered, about 5 minutes. Add about ¾ cup of stock, baking potatoes, and chard stems. Cover; cook over low heat until vegetables are almost tender, about 8 minutes.

Tear chard leaves and lettuce into bite-size pieces. Add with sweet potato, and spices to potato mixture. Cover and cook over low heat, stirring once, until sweet potato is almost tender, almost 8 minutes.

Add remaining 7¼ cups of stock and chicken to vegetables. Simmer until tender and chicken is heated through, about 5 minutes. Correct seasoning. Let stand for about 15 minutes before serving.

Serves 6 to 8

First
Courses

Opposite: Baked Crabmeat with Peach Salsa.
Above: Enchiladas. Below: Crawfish and Oyster
Pie. Right: Leeks Niçoise.

First Courses

Baked Crabmeat with Peach Salsa

Baked crabmeat cakes are one of everyone's favorites. They are related to that other crowd-pleasing favorite, crab cakes. Crabmeat is particularly delicious with a salsa made with peaches, but if they don't look too good when you get around to making this, you can substitute pears.

    1 pound backfin lump crabmeat
    3 tablespoons unsalted butter
    ½ cup finely chopped onions
    ½ cup finely chopped celery
    1 garlic clove, minced
    ½ cup chopped green onion tops
    2 tablespoons minced fresh parsley
    ⅓ cup mayonnaise
      Pinch of cayenne (ground red) pepper
    ¼ teaspoon black pepper
    1 teaspoon dry mustard
    ¼ teaspoon baking soda
    1 teaspoon salt
    1½ cups fresh saltine cracker crumbs

Preheat oven to 450 degrees.

Carefully pick over and drain the crabmeat. Set aside. Melt butter in a medium skillet over medium heat. Sauté onions, celery, garlic, and green onion tops until wilted, about 5 minutes. Do not brown. Remove from heat and stir in parsley and then the crabmeat. Mix mayonnaise, peppers, mustard, baking soda, and salt. Stir into the crabmeat mixture. Mix in ⅓ cup of the cracker crumbs.

Form into 12 medium patties and roll in remaining crumbs. Place in a well-oiled or buttered pan and bake for 10 minutes. Turn and bake for another 15 minutes.

Serve with Peach Salsa on the side (recipe follows).

Serves 6

PEACH SALSA

    3 firm medium peaches (about 1 pound)
    1 tablespoon fresh lemon juice
    2 ripe medium tomatoes (about ½ pound)
    6 large green onions
    1 tablespoon chopped canned jalapeño peppers
    1 tablespoon coarsely chopped cilantro (fresh
      coriander) (optional)

    12 tablespoons good-quality olive oil
     6 tablespoons sherry vinegar
     2 tablespoons honey

Dip peaches into boiling water and then peel the skins. Cut peaches into thin strips, discarding pits. Toss with lemon juice.

Dip tomatoes into boiling water and peel and seed them. Cut into medium julienne strips.

Combine peaches and tomatoes. Add onions, peppers, and cilantro, if using. Mix. Whisk together oil, vinegar, and honey. Pour over other ingredients.

You may leave this unrefrigerated if you are using it within several hours; otherwise, cover and refrigerate.

Makes approximately 2 cups

Leeks Niçoise

Leeks prepared this way look as appetizing as they taste.

    1 cup safflower oil
    1 cup olive oil
    3 tablespoons minced garlic
    2 tablespoons dried thyme leaves
    1 tablespoon black pepper
    6 medium leeks, *carefully* washed, halved, and
      trimmed to 8 inches
    1½ cups Chicken Stock (page 74), heated
    1 pint cherry tomatoes, stemmed, washed, and
      dried
    1 cup drained niçoise olives
    2 teaspoons salt

Warm oils in a large skillet with a lid. Stir in garlic, thyme, and pepper. Allow to warm for about 5 minutes to flavor the oils. Do not cook.

Place leeks in the oil. (If there is not room for them all, place excess on top of the bottom layer and fit them in as the leeks wilt. Cover tightly and simmer over low heat for 10 minutes. Turn with tongs and add chicken stock. Cover again, increase heat to medium, and simmer until tender, another 10 minutes. Remove leeks to a serving tray, folding green part under.

Add tomatoes, olives, and salt to the skillet and sauté over medium heat for about 3 minutes, shaking the pan gently to heat the tomatoes and olives but not mash the tomatoes.

Pour over leeks and serve at room temperature.

Serves 6

Enchiladas

Sauce

- 2 large red bell peppers
- 2 pounds very ripe tomatoes
- 6 medium garlic cloves
- 1 pound onions, coarsely chopped
- ¼ cup safflower oil
- 4 teaspoons ground cumin
- 1 teaspoon chili powder
- 1 teaspoon dried oregano
- 1 cup Chicken Stock (page 74)
- 1 large bay leaf
- 1 tablespoon salt, or to taste
- 1 teaspoon black pepper
- ⅛ teaspoon cayenne (ground red) pepper, or to taste

Filling

- 1 cup coarsely chopped onions
- 3 tablespoons unsalted butter
- 2½ cups grated Monterey Jack cheese
- 1 (11-ounce) can medium-hot green chilies, drained and chopped
- 1 cup sour cream
- 1 teaspoon salt

Assembly

- 12 flour tortillas
- 2 cups grated cheddar cheese

To make the sauce, place peppers, tomatoes, and garlic under the broiler. Turn as the skins blacken (remove garlic, since it will blacken first).

Sauté onions in oil until wilted. Stir in spices.

Scrape skin from red peppers and remove seeds; chop and add to onions. Skin tomatoes and coarsely chop; add to onion-pepper mixture. Snip ends off garlic and squeeze pulp into mixture. Stir.

Add stock, bay leaf, salt, and peppers. Simmer over medium-low heat for 20 minutes. Remove bay leaf and process mixture in a food processor to a lumpy texture.

To make filling, sauté onions in butter until wilted. Stir in cheese, chilies, sour cream, and salt.

To assemble enchiladas, first preheat oven to 350 degrees. Grease a shallow 9 × 13-inch casserole.

Divide filling among steamed tortillas and roll up. Cover the bottom of casserole with a bit of sauce. Place filled tortillas in dish. Cover with additional sauce, and top with the grated cheddar. Bake until cheese melts and mixture is bubbly, about 15 minutes.

Serves 6

Crawfish and Oyster Pie

If crawfish is not available, substitute shrimp.

Poaching Liquid

- 1 rib celery, chopped with leaves
- 1 medium onion, chopped
- 2 bay leaves
- 1 medium carrot, chopped
- 1 large sprig parsley
- 3 cups water
- 18 to 24 oysters, shucked

Filling

- 1 cup diced onions
- ¾ cup diced celery
- 1 teaspoon minced garlic
- 1½ tablespoons minced fresh parsley
- 2 teaspoons dried thyme
- 5 tablespoons unsalted butter
- ¼ cup all-purpose flour
- 3 tablespoons milk or cream
- 1 teaspoon salt, or to taste
- ½ teaspoon black pepper
  Pinch of cayenne (ground red) pepper
- 1 medium sweet potato, baked and cubed
- 1 pound frozen crawfish tails, thawed

Top Crust

  Pastry (use ½ recipe for Onion-Bacon Pie crust on page 59)
  Egg glaze (1 egg beaten with 3 tablespoons water)

For poaching liquid, combine celery, onion, bay leaves, carrot, parsley, and water. Simmer for a few minutes. Add oysters and poach over low heat for 2 minutes. Remove with a slotted spoon and set aside, lightly covered with wax paper. Strain liquid, reserving 2 cups.

Preheat oven to 425 degrees. Butter an 8-inch casserole.

For filling, sauté onions, celery, garlic, parsley, and thyme in butter until wilted. Do not brown. Add flour and cook until golden, mixing all the while. Add reserved poaching liquid, whisking. Simmer, whisking, for 3 minutes as sauce thickens. Add milk or cream, salt, pepper, and cayenne; cook for another 5 minutes.

Carefully fold in oysters, sweet potato, and crawfish. Pour into casserole and top with pastry. Seal edges with egg glaze and brush top with same. Make air slits in top and bake for 15 minutes. Turn heat back to 350 and bake for an additional 15 minutes.

Serves 6 to 8

Breads

Left to right: Rice Muffins, Jalapeño Corn Muffins, Caraway Cheese Muffins, Ham Bottom Rolls.

Breads

Rice Muffins

The rice in these muffins gives them a nice chewy texture.

1½ cups medium rye flour
½ cup all-purpose flour
1½ teaspoons baking powder
¼ teaspoon baking soda
 Pinch of cayenne (ground red) pepper
⅔ cup coarsely chopped green onions, with some tops
⅔ cup coarsely chopped celery
6 tablespoons (¾ stick) unsalted butter
2 cups cooked white rice, drained well
5 eggs, lightly beaten
½ cup water

Preheat oven to 400 degrees. Generously grease 12 medium muffin cups.

Sift together the flours, baking powder, baking soda, and cayenne.

Sauté the green onions and celery in the butter until wilted, about five minutes. Toss in the rice.

Mix the eggs and water. Stir into the dry mixture; do not overmix. Fold in the vegetables and rice. Spoon into cups until three-fourths full.

Bake for 20 minutes or until golden.

Makes 12 muffins

Jalapeño Corn Muffins

If hot peppers are not to your taste, substitute the canned, mild variety.

1½ cups yellow cornmeal
1 cup all-purpose flour
1 tablespoon baking powder
1 teaspoon chili powder
1 teaspoon ground cumin
½ teaspoon paprika
1 (17-ounce) can creamed corn
¼ cup chopped pickled jalapeño peppers, without seeds
¼ cup safflower oil or bacon fat
¼ cup milk
2 eggs, lightly beaten
4 ounces Monterey Jack, grated, or muenster cheese

Preheat oven to 400 degrees. Generously grease 12 large or 24 medium muffin cups.

In a large bowl sift together the cornmeal, flour, baking powder, chili powder, cumin, and paprika. In another bowl, mix thoroughly the creamed corn, peppers, oil, milk, and eggs. Combine with the dry ingredients; do not overmix. Fold in cheese and fill cups three-fourths full.

Bake until golden on top, about 20 minutes.

Makes 12 large or 24 medium muffins

Caraway Cheese Muffins

A good substitute here would be rye (with caraway seeds) cheese toast. You'd get almost the same flavor.

> 2 cups all-purpose flour
> 3 teaspoons baking powder
> 1½ teaspoons salt
> ¾ teaspoon black pepper
> 2 tablespoons caraway seeds
> 1 cup milk
> 2 eggs
> 2 tablespoons safflower oil
> 8 ounces sharp cheddar cheese, cubed

Preheat oven to 400 degrees. Generously grease 12 medium muffin cups.

Sift together the flour, baking powder, salt, and pepper. Stir in the caraway seeds. Beat together the milk, eggs, and oil. Combine with the dry ingredients; do not overmix. Fold in the cheese. Fill cups to three-fourths full.

Bake for 15 minutes or until golden.

Makes 12 muffins

Ham Bottom Rolls

This dough can be kept in the refrigerator for about a week and used as needed. You can bake it as is, or make ham rolls out of it as follows.

> 2 cups warm water (105–115°F)
> 3 tablespoons sugar
> 2 packages active dry yeast
> 1½ teaspoons salt
> 1 egg, well beaten
> 3 tablespoons safflower oil
> 2 cups all-purpose flour
> 3 cups whole wheat flour
> Thin sliced prosciutto, coarsely chopped

Place warm water in the work bowl of an electric mixer fitted with a dough hook. Stir in sugar and sprinkle yeast over all. Stir to mix before adding salt, egg, and oil. Mix in flours until dough becomes very hard to stir, adding more flour if necessary.

Knead dough for 6 to 7 minutes with the dough hook, adding more flour if it is still too damp. It should become smooth and elastic.

Scrape into a lightly greased bowl and cover with plastic wrap. Allow to rise in a warm, draft-free spot until doubled in bulk, about 40 minutes to an hour.

When doubled, punch down with floured plastic wrap; refrigerate until ready to use.

Pinch off walnut-size pieces of dough and flatten each. Press some of the chopped prosciutto into the center. Form into a ball again, enclosing the meat, and flatten very slightly. Place on a greased cookie sheet and cover with a tea towel in a warm spot.

Bake for 20 minutes or until light brown.

Makes approximately 60 small rolls

Desserts

Opposite: Baked Stuffed Pears with Vanilla Sauce.
Right: Butterscotch Pecan Cookies with Butterscotch
Pecan Ice Cream. Below, left: Apple Sorbet.
Below, right: White Chocolate Tarts with Dark
Chocolate Cream.

Desserts

Apple Sorbet

Don't be fooled by the fact that this recipe looks so simple. It is that of course, but it is also delicious.

    4 small tart apples, peeled, cored, and quartered
    1 cup water
    ⅔ cup sugar
    2 teaspoons lemon juice
      Calvados or other apple brandy (optional)

Place all ingredients except the brandy in a medium saucepan and simmer until apples are tender, about 10 minutes. Purée in a food processor and allow to cool.

Freeze in an ice-cream freezer according to manufacturer's directions.

Make an indentation in the top of each serving with the back of a spoon and fill with apple brandy.

May be served with a sugar wafer, if desired.

Makes approximately 1 quart

Baked Stuffed Pears with Vanilla Sauce

The ubiquitous pear is always dependable for making cold-weather desserts. The recipe for the vanilla sauce served with this is good and simple. However, any one would do. If you have a recipe of which you are particularly fond, by all means use it.

    3 large pears, peeled, cut in half, and cored
      Lemon juice
    ⅓ cup raisins or dried currants
    3 tablespoons sugar
    2 tablespoons (¼ stick) unsalted butter
    1 tablespoon cognac (optional)
    2 teaspoons ground cinnamon
    ½ teaspoon grated nutmeg

Preheat oven to 400 degrees. Generously grease a baking dish into which pear halves will fit snugly.

Rub pear halves generously with lemon juice (to keep from discoloring) and set aside.

Grind or chop the raisins very fine and mix with the other ingredients to make a paste. Fill each pear cavity with the mixture. Place pears, filled side down, in baking dish. Bake until tender, about 30 minutes. Allow to cool slightly, then carefully remove with a spatula.

Serve warm on a pool of warm Vanilla Sauce (recipe follows). Pass additional sauce, if desired.

Serves 6

VANILLA SAUCE

    2 cups milk
    1 vanilla bean
    2 egg yolks
    ⅓ cup sugar
    1 tablespoon cornstarch

Place milk and vanilla bean in a saucepan and bring slowly to a simmer. Meanwhile, beat together the yolks, sugar, and cornstarch. Stir into the hot milk off the heat. Return saucepan to low heat and cook another few minutes, whisking all the while, until mixture thickens slightly.

Set aside and remove bean, scraping seeds out into the sauce before serving.

Makes a generous 2 cups

Butterscotch Pecan Cookies

Several years ago I received a very nice letter from a lady who had been given one of my books as a gift. In her letter she remarked on how much she liked cookies for dessert and how glad she was to see that I shared her enthusiasm. With the letter she enclosed a favorite cookie recipe of hers. And here it is. Unfortunately, along the way her typed letter lost its last page with her name. So if you read this, many thanks. I'm glad others may now enjoy this cookie as much as we both have.

    ½ cup (1 stick) unsalted butter
    1 cup dark brown sugar, tightly packed
    1 large egg
    ½ cup finely chopped pecans
    ½ teaspoon vanilla extract
    1½ cups all-purpose flour
    ½ teaspoon salt
    ½ teaspoon baking powder
    ¼ teaspoon baking soda

Cream the butter and sugar until smooth. Add the egg and pecans. Mix thoroughly, then stir in vanilla. Set aside while you sift the remaining ingredients together. Combine well with the butter-sugar mixture.

On a floured surface, divide the dough in half (this will be very sticky). Shape a roll from each half that is about 2 inches in diameter and wrap securely with plastic. Refrigerate for at least 1 hour, more if you have time.

Preheat oven to 350 degrees.

Cut chilled dough into thin ⅛-inch slices. Place 1 inch apart on an ungreased cookie sheet and bake until cookies are golden but not browned, about 15 to 16 minutes. Remove with a spatula while warm. Place on a rack to cool.

These cookies are wonderful served with butter pecan ice cream.

Makes about 3 dozen cookies

White Chocolate Tarts with Dark Chocolate Cream

This is a very rich dessert, so you might want to cut this recipe in half and just serve 1 tart to each guest garnished with a few strawberries.

Tartlet Crust
  ¾ cup solid vegetable shortening
  ¼ cup boiling water
  1 teaspoon salt
  1 tablespoon milk
     Approximately 2 cups sifted all-purpose flour

White Chocolate Filling
  6 ounces white chocolate, coarsely chopped
  ¼ cup superfine sugar
  1 large egg yolk, room temperature
  ½ teaspoon vanilla extract
  2 tablespoons instant espresso
  1 cup heavy cream
  2 large egg whites
     Pinch of salt

Chocolate Whipped Cream
  1 ounce unsweetened chocolate
  4 tablespoons sugar
  1 cup whipping cream

To make crust, place shortening in a large bowl and pour the boiling water over it. Stir to melt and make a smooth mixture. Add the salt and milk, and stir to mix. Add the flour, ½ cup at a time, mixing well after each addition, until you have added 1½ cups. After that, add flour just until the mixture clings together and makes a stiff dough. Form into a ball, flatten between 2 sheets of wax paper, and refrigerate for at least 1 hour.

Preheat the oven to 350 degrees.

Roll out dough on a floured surface. Press the dough into 12 individual 2-inch tart tins. Line the tins with foil, pressing well into the bottom corners, and weight with beans, rice, or aluminum or ceramic weights. Bake for 15 to 18 minutes. When the pastry begins to color around the edges, remove the foil and weights and continue to bake just until the pastry dries out and turns golden. Let cool completely before filling.

To make white chocolate filling, melt white chocolate chunks in the top of a double boiler until almost liquid, leaving some lumps. Stir in sugar and allow to cool slightly. Stir in egg yolk, vanilla extract, and 1 tablespoon of the instant espresso. Set aside.

Whip cream and refrigerate. Whip the egg whites with the pinch of salt until they form stiff peaks. Fold into the white chocolate filling, then fold in the whipped cream, adding the other tablespoon of instant espresso at the end. Do not overmix. Refrigerate.

To make chocolate whipped cream, place chocolate, sugar, and 2 tablespoons of cream in the top of a double boiler. When the chocolate is melted, whip until cooled and set aside. Whip the rest of the cream and add it to the chocolate. Mix just enough to thicken but not stiffen.

On individual plates, place 2 small tart shells each on a slick of chocolate cream and fill each with the white chocolate filling. More instant espresso may be sprinkled over each just before serving, if you like.

Serves 6

SOME GOOD SANDWICHES

You know, I have found that every time I get involved in a project that is new to me, I later find something in it that I hadn't realized was there when I started. Take writing for instance. And writing about food in particular. Like many other people, there are things about almost *everything* that bug me. I don't think there is anything especially weird about that. However, the difference for me now is that I can get some if it off my chest by writing about them; and I have discovered—through letters and conversations—that there are always some like-minded souls out there.

Well, we are on the subject of sandwiches. You know what I hate? I hate those things they call "overstuffed" sandwiches. I mean, if I wanted to eat a few pounds of sliced roast beef or ham, that's what I'd order. Why bother calling it a sandwich? Or, at the other end of the scale, what about those places that make so-called sandwiches on half a loaf of Italian or French bread. Bread sandwiches. Who wants that? So what I'm getting at here is balance. The balance between the bread and what it encloses.

I can't tell you how much better I feel for getting this out in the open.

So there are some suggestions for types of what I call real sandwiches, which you might enjoy with soups. Obviously, there is plenty of room for expressing personal preferences here. And that you should certainly do. The point is that you may not have thought of, or have forgotten about, some of the combinations I suggest.

Oh yes, I've remembered one other thing I don't like: it's about the way sandwiches are sometimes presented. Like when a sandwich is all laid out, opened up, to display its ingredients as if it's for some picture. Personally, these make me think of those exploded mechanical drawings that diagram the various parts of a piece of machinery; or worse, of a dog that has rolled over on its back to show you it is friendly. Fine for a dog, bad for a sandwich. I want mine (sandwich, not dog) the way the Earl of Sandwich intended it to be. Hold the presentation and slice it, please. Diagonally preferably, but I'm agreeable if you want to cut it in half the other way.

I'm not a sorehead. I'm observant.

To tell you the truth, it didn't seem to make much sense for me to start giving specific quantities of ingredients for making sandwiches. After all, they are—or should be by their very nature—quick and easy to prepare and very personal, including as much of any one ingredient as you like. You are the boss here.

With that in mind I have divided this section rather arbitrarily into groupings of foods that relate to one another.

Sandwich Spreads

When you think about it, you can make a sandwich spread from almost anything that will stick together. And I think this category is one that is often overlooked. A paste or spread of some sort can be made in advance and often keeps well in the refrigerator. So it's there for you to use on short notice. Of course, the advent of the food processor has made the task of preparation all the easier.

The following is a collection of the spreads I use, but which I hope will be a starting point for you to come up with spreads that may more accurately reflect your own personal tastes.

Of course, many variations may be made simply by using different breads with different spreads. If the bread is cut thick, make them open-face.

Cucumber

As you might imagine, the cucumbers give this a very refreshing flavor. However, you must work on it to ensure that it isn't too bland.

> Cucumbers
> Salt
> Pot (or cottage) cheese
> Mayonnaise or light cream
> Tabasco
> Grated onion
> Worcestershire sauce
> Paprika
> Freshly ground black pepper
> Crumbled crisp bacon

Peel and seed the cucumbers, then cut into medium chunks. Sprinkle generously with salt and place in the refrigerator for several hours, covered. Remove and drain. Discard liquid and dry the chunks between paper towels. Mince the cucumbers. Meanwhile, mix the pot cheese with just enough mayonnaise or cream to make it spreadable. Season with Tabasco, grated onion, Worcestershire, paprika, and pepper (no salt needed). Stir in the cucumbers and bacon just before using.

Smoked Salmon

Who ever has leftover smoked salmon? Well, just in case.

> Smoked salmon
> Chopped fresh dill
> Cream cheese
> Light cream
> Salt and pepper to taste
> Fresh lemon juice

Purée the salmon, chopped dill, cream cheese, and just enough cream to help with the texture. Taste the mixture at this point before adding the other ingredients. And don't go too heavy on the dill because you want the fish to predominate.

Caviar

This is a pretty glamourous sandwich spread, but what the heck.
When made slightly ahead of time, the caviar will color the cream cheese, either pinkish or gray-blue, depending on the type of caviar you use.

> Light cream
> Fresh lemon juice
> Cream cheese
> Caviar
> Chopped fresh chives

This should be mixed by hand. Use the cream and lemon juice to soften the cream cheese just to the point of its being spreadable. Fold in the caviar and chives. Don't mash.

Grilled Tuna with Roasted Peppers

This is a good use for leftover grilled tuna steak (or swordfish).

> Grilled tuna steak or tuna packed in oil, drained
> Mayonnaise
> Sour cream
> Roasted red bell pepper, seeded and peeled
> Fresh lemon juice
> Salt and pepper to taste

You can make this into a paste by puréeing all the ingredients in a food processor, except for the lemon juice, salt, and pepper, which you can add last. The proportion of mayonnaise to sour cream should be about 3 to 1. Store this in the refrigerator with a sheet of wax paper pressed onto the top until ready to use.

Lima Bean

This is another good use for a leftover. Use baked dried limas.

> Baked dried lima beans, well drained
> Chopped watercress
> Mayonnaise
> Fresh lemon juice
> Tabasco
> Minced green onions

The best way to do this is to purée the cooked beans and chopped watercress first. Taste it at this point before adding the mayonnaise and lemon juice, because you may not need much of either. Ditto with the Tabasco, which should be mixed with the mayonnaise if you are using it. Stir in the green onions just before you use the spread.

Ham

> Baked ham cut from the bone
> Mayonnaise
> Dijon mustard
> Prepared horseradish (optional)
> Sweet pickle relish

Precooked ham that is then baked before being used improves in flavor considerably, so I would advise doing this. It doesn't require much in the way of preparation otherwise. Grind the ham to whatever consistency you like (I think it shouldn't be made into a paste, but that is my own preference), then mix a little mustard into the mayonnaise to taste. Fold this in thoroughly. Taste to see if you need more. If you are going to use horseradish, it should be added to the mayonnaise-mustard mix. Add the relish last, mixing well. This is one of those spreads that doesn't require many ingredients. I prefer a generous amount of mayonnaise with just a hint of mustard. After all, the mustard can be put on the bread if you want more.

Grilled Sandwiches

Like most of us, I love grilled sandwiches. And I have a little trick I use when making them, which, though obvious, makes them easier to do. Spread one side of a slice of bread with soft butter and place it, butter side down, in a cold skillet. Put the filling on top and then top with another slice of buttered bread, buttered side up. Go on from there, grilling it over medium heat.

I also like my grilled sandwiches on very thin bread, so that the bread doesn't dominate. First, the classic.

Cheeses

1. Butter
   Very thin slices of whole wheat bread
   Honey mustard
   Emmenthal cheese

Spread butter on bread as just described and spread the other side with honey mustard. Top with cheese and a final slice of bread. Start in a cold skillet over medium heat. Serve with cornichons.

More Suggestions:

2. Butter
   Very thin slices of whole wheat bread
   Mild chèvre (goat) cheese
   Prosciutto slices

3. Butter
   Very thin slices of white bread
   Mozzarella cheese slices
   Roasted bell pepper (see Extras, page 145)

4. Butter
   Very thin slices of white bread
   Swiss cheese slices
   Wilted cucumbers (see Extras, page 145)
   Strips of crisp bacon

5. Butter
   Very thin slices of soft rye bread
   Green peppercorn mustard
   Sharp cheddar cheese slices
   Wilted green onions (see Extras, page 145)

6. Butter
   Very thin slices of soft rye bread
   Mashed blue cheese
   Chopped walnuts

Peanut Butter Variations

I always use chunky peanut butter whenever I make grilled sandwiches.

1. Butter
   Thin slices of white bread
   Chunky peanut butter
   Thin slices of red onion

Spread butter on one side of both bread slices as described earlier, and spread the other side of 1 slice with a layer of peanut butter. Place buttered side down in a cold skillet. Top with onion slice and the other buttered slice. Grill over medium heat.

More Suggestions:

2. Butter
   Thin slices of whole wheat bread
   Chunky peanut butter
   Strips of crisp bacon

3. Butter
   Thin slices of whole wheat bread
   Chunky peanut butter
   Fig preserves, drained and chopped

Breads

You have a tremendous selection in this category, so take advantage of it. There seem to be new kinds of bread every time I go into the specialty stores. Along with the traditional white, whole wheat, and rye, you now regularly see sourdough, English muffin white, nut breads of every kind, cheese bread, and breads with every imaginable addition, from onions to tomatoes, from herbs to olives. Buy yourself a good serrated knife and go to it. Just remember not to cut the bread so thick that it overpowers what it is enclosing.

Flavored Butters

This is another one of those categories that adapts itself to endless variations. You merely need a little softened butter and imagination. The taste of the butter may be altered or enhanced before other ingredients are added by whipping in, very judiciously, a bit of mustard, pepper, drops of Tabasco, fresh lemon juice, or horseradish. When doing this, remember that the point is not to overwhelm the flavor of the butter, but to embellish it. Incidentally, you may use good homemade mayonnaise instead of butter in many cases.

To the basic butter add any combination of fresh herbs you particularly like the flavor of, or just a single herb. For instance, chopped fresh parsley or chives make a marvelous beginning for classic tea sandwiches. Or for meat sandwiches, how about butter flavored with minced shallots?

Anything goes.

Then there are butters that are made with a reduction of wine and herbs, which is then whipped into the butter. For instance, the onions can first be wilted in the least bit of butter, then covered with red wine which is allowed to simmer until onions are very soft and the wine has almost evaporated. This butter is often flavorful enough to just spread between two very thin slices of bread with a little fresh pepper (I'd cut off the crusts) and eaten as is.

Fresh Meat Fillings

Some time ago I got onto keeping thin-sliced uncooked meats (not cold cuts) in the refrigerator on weekends in case I wanted sandwiches for lunch. I began with veal and then went on to pounded chicken breast and now sliced turkey breast. These are all delicious and may be prepared in the same way. Here's how you do it.

The uncooked meat should be thin, so if it isn't, pound it between 2 sheets of wax paper. Salt, pepper, and flour each piece, shaking off excess. Then dip in beaten egg, allowing excess to drain off before coating with bread crumbs. Fry until golden in a mixture of butter and oil. This won't take too long, and be careful not to burn the coating. When I do this, I set up a regular assembly line next to the stove. On a sheet of wax paper is the flour, then a flat plate with the beaten egg, and finally, a sheet of wax paper to hold the fresh, soft bread crumbs.

There are, as you can imagine, variations here, too. For instance, instead of soft bread crumbs, you might use cracker crumbs or a combination of the two. You might also add grated Parmesan cheese, chives, parsley, or a favored herb to this mix.

These breaded cutlets can be cooked hours in advance of when they'll be used. Drain them well and cover with a tea towel.

And in a pinch you can even freeze the uncooked slices. This doesn't exactly improve their texture and flavor, but since you are doing a lot to alter both in this particular preparation, that is not so important as it would be in, say, veal scallopini.

So you see that the sandwich is a wonderfully varied category of food as an accompaniment to soup—making, to many people, such a perfectly satisfying and nutritious meal that it's no wonder the combination has become so very popular over the years that people often think of the two—soup and sandwich—as a match made in heaven. Maybe it was.

Extras

When people want a little extra crunch in their sandwich, they often stop with lettuce (and iceberg, at that). Now, frankly I've got nothing against iceberg lettuce. After all, I grew up on it and still like its cool texture in a sandwich. But it simply has almost no flavor. So what about adding a little watercress or arugula for instance? Or how about strips of endive or radicchio?

I might as well confess that there is one addition I think is an invention of the devil—or the sixties, or both: sprouts. Whenever I see them, either on a sandwich or in a salad, I know it's likely I've wandered into the wrong place. I'm sure this will probably bring down the wrath of The National Sprout Growers Coalition for a Heathier America, or some such, but I cannot tell a lie. But like everything else, there is an exception. I love radish sprouts.

Then, instead of those tasteless winter tomatoes, try substituting sun-dried or sliced cherry tomatoes, which usually have more flavor.

Wilted cucumbers and onions add both flavor and texture, and I love strips of roasted peppers on sandwiches.

• Cucumbers can be wilted simply by putting them, peeled and sliced, into a bowl generously sprinkled with salt and then placing a weight on top. The salt will draw out much of the liquid after a few hours and can be poured off. You can also sprinkle the layers with chopped fresh dill before weighting.

• Onions—sweet, red, or green—can be sliced and placed in a bowl, then a mixture of one part each water, oil, vinegar, and one-eighth part sugar that has been brought to the boiling point can be poured over. You can also add a little salt, pepper, and Tabasco to the marinade. Cover and refrigerate after the liquid has cooled.

• To roast sweet peppers, place them in a foil-lined pan and blacken under a broiler, turning as each side blackens. Place them in a small paper bag and close the top. Allow to cool before removing skin and seeds. Cut in large strips and store covered with olive oil.

EQUIPMENT AND SOURCES

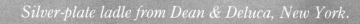

Silver-plate ladle from Dean & Deluca, New York.

One of the pluses of making soup is that the doing doesn't really call for much in the way of special equipment. As a matter of fact, most moderately well equipped kitchens will likely already include the needed utensils. However, the required inventory is worth reviewing because, as is so often the case, the right equipment can make preparation easier and more efficient.

Another aspect of soup making, which people often don't seem to consider, is that many soups freeze well. So it follows that you should be prepared with the proper freezer containers. Such storage equipment need not be fancy or expensive—just available when you need or want it. And while you are buying, don't forget to include a few small stackable freezer containers for individual servings. These are really handy. Also remember to have labels and marking pencils.

Personally, I am always squirreling away containers other food has come in, so I have them to use when I want to give some leftovers to a guest to take home and they won't have to worry about getting the container back to me. This goes for individual servings as well as large.

OK, you've got the soup made, but what is it going to be served in (and with)? Why should you limit your options here? Soup can be presented in a number of ways. It looks quite appetizing in a large tureen on the end of the table, but this needn't be a conventional tureen. For instance, I like glass cylinders to serve soup from, especially in the summer, or a large pitcher. Or any sort of crockery bowl with a fairly decent capacity can be pressed into service. And don't forget the soup ladle. Remember that a ladle doesn't necessarily always have to be made from anything as serious as sterling silver; they come in everything from tin to ceramic.

And don't overlook the soup spoons themselves. Europeans tend toward spoons that seem oversized to many of us. I like the look of them, but prefer something just one step down in size. However, I don't think it is really necessary to have both regular and cream soup spoons, unless you care for formal entertaining.

Finally, as for individual soup plates and bowls, I'm partial to rather flat, rimmed soup plates. These are especially good if you are having a hearty soup that includes meat that will need cutting, or bones from which you want to extract the marrow at the table.

Then there are times when oversized cups may be utilized, or even large, low glasses, as when you are serving a cold soup. Here again, give yourself a little variety if you plan to have soup often, and have the storage place for extra dinnerware.

Let me say, while we are on the subject, that as much as I like the way some individual covered soup bowls look when the soup is presented, I find having to deal with the top once it is removed at the table rather awkward, so on balance I think I'd skip them.

Now, as to the basic equipment. First, you will want to have nice stockpots if you intend to make your own stock. I would buy two sizes in a good, heavy-duty metal—and don't forget the lids.

You will also need an assortment of good stirring and skimming spoons, both wooden and metal.

Strainers and colanders are other items that you will want to have. You'll find you use them over and over again. And in this vein, get yourself a couple of good slotted or straining spoons for lifting out solid ingredients. Also for serving, be sure to equip yourself with several sizes of kitchen ladles.

Should you not have a food processor, and not intend to purchase one, you will need some other piece of equipment to purée with. There are a number of options from which to choose, ranging from hand ricers to large food mills. Frankly, I am so accustomed to using a food processor and I use it so often when making soups, that I think I'd be lost without it. And they get the job done so fast. In that case, you will want to have several sizes of rubber spatulas for scraping the puréed food from the processor bowl.

Speaking of spatulas, you will require a flat-ended metal one (a pancake turner) when you make roux.

You'll obviously need a good can opener from time to time, but I can't imagine a kitchen not having one. However, when it comes to preparing the vegetables, which are incorporated into most soups in one way or another, I'm amazed at how few people invest in good paring knives, especially since these seem so basic to me. Plan to buy several sizes if you don't have any. And for the knives, buy a sharpener. There is nothing as maddening as a dull blade, especially when there are such good and easy-to-use sharpeners around these days. Also, for vegetables, you'll need the old reliable potato peeler.

I find I am constantly using cutting and chopping boards in soup making, too. One of the handiest ones is a small board on which I mince garlic and the like. You'll want different sizes anyway. I use both wood and plastic.

You might also want to have a timer that you can carry with you as a reminder to check the pot if you are allowing something to simmer for a long period. I do this. I also find I use tongs very often to fish out solid ingredients.

So, as I said at the beginning, many of you will have some or all of this equipment in your kitchen already. Use this as a check list.

*Paderno stainless steel stockpot from Dean &
Deluca; Rubbermaid spatula, stainless steel slotted
spoon, ladles, tongs, and Teraillon kitchen timer
from Dean & Deluca and many other gourmet shops
and housewares stores. Chantry knife sharpener
from Lee Bailey at Saks Fifth Avenue, New York,
and selected branches.*

Wooden spoons and cutting board; stainless steel
mesh strainer, colander, perforated skimmer, mesh
skimmer; Mouli stainless steel food mill, all from
Dean & Deluca and many other gourmet shops and
housewares stores.

*From left: Covered soup tureen and ceramic ladle
from Wolfman-Gold; Austrian ceramic wide-rim
bowl and open glass storage jar from Dean &
Deluca; pitcher and glass bowl from author's own
collection; French porcelain bowl with bistro orange
stripe from Dean & Deluca.*

Clockwise from upper left: Rosenthal china soup bowls from Bloomingdale's and other department stores; large ceramic cup and saucer from Lee Bailey at Saks Fifth Avenue; porcelain bistro bowl, Pillivuyt soup bowl, and bouillon cup and saucer from Dean & Deluca; Mexican bowl from author's own collection. Center: Tumbler from Lee Bailey at Saks Fifth Avenue.

From left: Helik stainless steel spoon from Lee Bailey at Saks Fifth Avenue; antique silver spoon; David Melor silver spoon and stainless steel spoon with white plastic handle from Lee Bailey at Saks Fifth Avenue; silver-plate dessert spoon from Dean & Deluca.

Assorted stackable freezer containers from many housewares stores.

Index

Acknowledgments

As always, my thanks and appreciation to everyone at my publishers, Clarkson N. Potter. The same to my designers, Rochelle Udell and Doug Turshen.

A very special word of thanks to the photographer on this project, Tom Eckerle. This marks the first time we have worked together, and it was a pleasure. I think you will agree that his pictures are simply beautiful.

Another very special word of thanks to my friend Tom Byrne, a brilliant and innovative cook, who just happened to be around this summer when I desperately needed a hand. Tom, you made it a breeze.

And to all the friends and acquaintances who so generously allowed me to photograph in their houses (and gardens): Jack Ceglic, Joel Dean, Loren Dunlap, Sean Driscoll, Mary Emmerling, Nora Ephron, Tom Fallon, Christopher Idone, Mr. and Mrs. John Laird, David Luck, Jennifer Patterson, Nick Pileggi, Mr. and Mrs. Ham Richardson, Jerome Robbins, and Howard Stringer.

Also thanks to Teresa and Tony Babinski, Dorothy Bates, C & W Mercantile (Bridgehampton), Judy Corman, Dean & Deluca, Ina Garten, Fleurette Gullioz, Peachy Halsey, Joan Muli, Jim Nelgrin, Pine Street Antiques (Southampton), and Peri Wolfman.

And to my dear, dear friend Carole Bannett, to whose memory this book is dedicated. She helped me right up until the end.